REYKJAVÍK

JENNA GOTTLIEB

Contents

Discover Reykjavík 4

The Best of Reykjavík 6

Reykjavík. 8

Background. 85

Essentials. 98

Resources. 111

Index 122

Clockwise from top left: window detail in the Harpa concert hall; pipe organ inside Hallgrímskirkja; autumn in Reykjavík; northern lights above Reykjavík.

Reykjavík is having a moment. Relatively affordable airfares are drawing weekenders from both sides of the Atlantic, giving Iceland's capital city a chance to show off its urban appeal and highly individualistic style.

With quaint museums, cool music venues, and top-notch restaurants, small Reykjavík makes a big impression. Stroll the capital's streets and explore the galleries, coffeehouses, intimate concert venues, and music shops—you can't help but feel the city's creative energy. Handcrafted local beers replace specialty coffees as the drink of choice come evening time, when low-key daytime hangouts morph into pulsing parties that fuel Reykjavík's thriving nightlife scene.

Clockwise from top left: example of Reykjavík's charm; Hallgrímskirkja doors; colorful downtown Reykjavík; Reykjavík during twilight blue hour; aerial view of Reykjavík.

The Best of Reykjavík

Day 1

Explore downtown Reykjavík and all the shops, galleries, restaurants, and coffeehouses the city has to offer. Walk down the street **Skólavörðustígur** to the landmark church **Hallgrímskirkja** to check out the amazing interior, beautiful organ, and view from the top. Grab coffee or lunch on Skólavörðustígur at **Café Babalu,** which makes tasty lattes and light meals like crepes and panini. The street is also where you can pick up a traditional Icelandic sweater at the **Handknitting Association of Iceland**.

Walk down the main street, **Laugavegur,** and pop into shops like **Hrím** for Icelandic design and **Mál og Menning** for books, T-shirts, and other tourist wares. Walk toward city hall and stroll around the manmade pond **Tjörnin,** where you can check out swans, ducks, and other birds that call the pond home.

For dinner, consider one of the city's trendy restaurants, like **Fiskfelagid** for the freshest catch of the day or **Buddha Café** for Asian fusion. Reykjavík nightlife is epic, and venues like **Húrra** and **Kex Hostel** are perfect to check out local DJs or live bands and to dance the night away.

Day 2

Reykjavík's harbor has a lot to see. Have breakfast at **Café Haiti** and watch boats enter the harbor. Sign up for a **whale-watching** or **bird-watching** excursion to have a chance to see minke whales, dolphins, fin whales, blue whales, and seabirds (depending on the season). Once back on land, take a walk over to the **Saga Museum** to learn about Iceland's history and enjoy a coffee and snack or light meal at the in-house café, **Kol & Salt.** Walk over

Reykjavík

Harpa concert hall

to **Harpa** concert hall to take in a concert or just check out the amazing interior and architecturally significant exterior.

Walk back downtown and check out the **Reykjavík Art Museum,** then have dinner at the wildly popular restaurant **Osushi**, which features delicious sushi. Stop by **Bar 11** to hear some local live music.

Day 3

Go to **Mokka** café on **Skólavörðustígur** for breakfast—the waffles with homemade jam and fresh cream are delightful. Visit Reykjavík's best record shops: Head to **12 Tónar,** a few stores up from Mokka, and then walk to **Lucky Records** near Hlemmur bus station.

Instead of going directly to the airport, sign up for a bus transfer to the **Blue Lagoon** to enjoy the glorious milky water. Then head to Keflavík for your flight.

soaking in the famous Blue Lagoon hot springs

Reykjavík

Sights 11

Sports and Recreation 24

Entertainment and Events 26

Shopping....................... 32

Accommodations............... 39

Food 44

Information and Services 53

Transportation................. 54

Greater Reykjavík.............. 57

Reykjanes Peninsula 66

The Golden Circle.............. 76

Though Reykjavík is small, its energy mimics that of New York City or Berlin.

Reykjavík residents are known to have two lives: They work by day and become musicians, artists, novelists, or poets by night. While strolling on Reykjavík's main street, Laugavegur, you'll see street art among the high-end shops, musicians playing impromptu concerts outside coffeehouses, and small art galleries boasting original "Icelandic Design." It's undeniably a creative place.

Reykjavík's history dates back to AD 874, when Ingólfur Arnarson from Norway established the first settlement in Iceland. The city slowly grew over the centuries, and in 1786, Reykjavík was established as an official trading town; 1786 is considered the city's official founding date. Today, Reykjavík has a lot of people, cars, and trees—in stark contrast to the rest of Iceland. Roughly 200,000 of Iceland's 330,000 residents live in the capital city.

While Reykjavík can seem quite urban with its galleries and restaurants, nature is never too far away. The air is unbelievably clean (unlike in many urban areas), and whales can be seen passing by the harbor during the summer.

Previous: downtown Reykjavík; a park near the Alþingishúsið.

Look for ★ to find recommended
sights, activities, dining, and lodging.

Highlights

★ **Listasafn Reykjavíkur (Reykjavík Art Museum):** It's actually three museums in one, with one dedicated to sculpture, one to contemporary art, and one that houses the works of beloved Icelandic artist Jóhannes Kjarval. If you buy a ticket to one museum, you can visit the other two on the same day (page 11).

★ **Hallgrímskirkja:** The "Church of Hallgrímur" is a striking national monument dedicated to Hallgrímur Pétursson, one of Iceland's most cherished and celebrated poets. Its tower offers spectacular views (page 16).

★ **Listasafn Íslands (National Gallery of Iceland):** The largest collection of Icelandic art on the island has everything from classic portraits to gorgeous landscapes (page 19).

★ **Tjörnin:** Close to Reykjavík City Hall, this pond is a lovely place to take a stroll and enjoy the birdlife (page 19).

★ **Harpa:** This striking concert hall features individual glass panels that light up during the darkness of winter (page 20).

★ **Sólfar (Sun Voyager):** The large Viking boat sculpture by the sea has been delighting photographers and tourists for decades (page 21).

★ **Perlan:** This unique dome-shaped building has one of the best views of the city, with an outdoor deck and huge mounted binoculars to check out the city below (page 23).

★ **Hiking Mount Esja:** The 914-meter-high Esja is perfect for hikers who don't have the time to venture far from the city. An easy climb on basalt rock climaxes with gorgeous views out to sea (page 57).

★ **Bláa Lónið (Blue Lagoon):** This gorgeous, geothermally heated spring heals the skin and soothes the body (page 71).

PLANNING YOUR TIME

Given its small size, Reykjavík can be "done" in 1-2 days depending on your level of interest. Some travelers treat Reykjavík as their starting point before heading out on the Ring Road or booking day trips into the countryside, while others travel to Reykjavík specifically for the nightlife and art scene.

ORIENTATION

Reykjavík is the most compact capital city in all of Europe. City center and the old harbor are situated in the northern half of the city, and the main bus station (BSÍ) is in the south. Most of the hotels, museums, shops, and restaurants are in the northern half, and tourists don't have to venture far outside city center on short trips to Reykjavík.

The main street in central Reykjavík is Laugavegur, which starts in the east. As you move west, it eventually becomes Bankastræti, which ends up Austurstræti. The streets tend to have long names, and there isn't a grid system in place, but the city is small enough that you won't get too lost. Hlemmur bus station on the east end of Laugavegur is Strætó's main depot downtown. It can connect you to just about anywhere in central and greater Reykjavík.

Sights

CENTRAL REYKJAVÍK
★ Listasafn Reykjavíkur (Reykjavík Art Museum)

The **Reykjavík Art Museum** is actually three museums (Hafnarhús, Kjarvalsstaðir, and Ásmundarsafn) in three different locations. Admission is 1,200ISK, and each museum is open 10am-5pm daily. It's important to note that if you purchase a ticket to any one of the three museums, you are granted free admission to the other two. But the free entry is only available on the same day your ticket was purchased. Each museum is pretty small and you can hit all three in one day, as an hour at each is enough time.

HAFNARHÚS

Hafnarhús (Tryggvagata 17, tel. 354/590-1200, www.listasafnreykjavikur. is), which focuses on contemporary art, is the crown jewel of the three museums, in part because of its permanent collection of Erró paintings and prints. Erró, an Icelandic pop artist, is one of the most celebrated modern Icelandic artists. The museum's collection is extensive, and works are regularly rotated to make room for new works. His work ranges from light pop art with bright colors and interesting characters to samples of line sketches from his earlier work. While the art can be playful, the artist also tackles political and social issues in his work. The museum also houses works from other Icelandic artists, as well as rotating exhibitions of foreign painters, designers, and visual artists. You get a sense that this is Reykjavík's version

Central Reykjavík

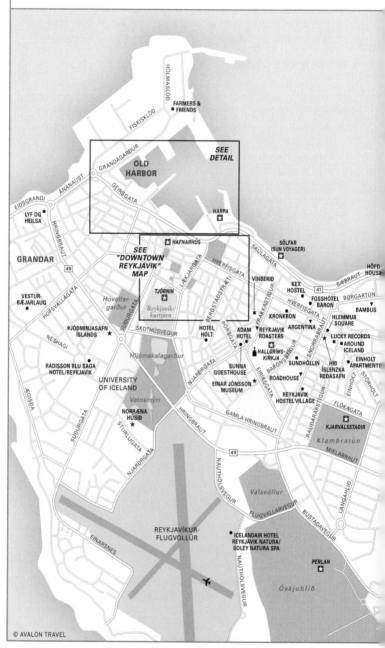

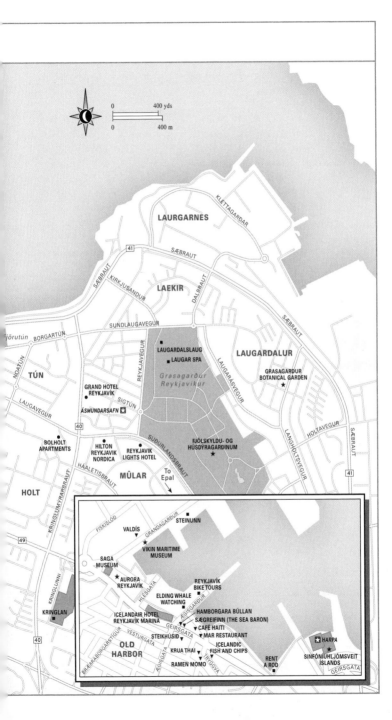

of New York's Museum of Modern Art. The museum is based in a nondescript white-block building, and the interior has three floors of exhibitions. The ground floor holds the souvenir shop and coat check along with a large open space for exhibits. The upper floors are dedicated to exhibitions.

KJARVALSSTAÐIR

Kjarvalsstaðir (Flókagata 24, tel. 354/517-1290, www.listasafnreykjavikur.is) is the place to go if you're looking to explore the works of Icelandic painter Jóhannes Kjarval (1885-1972), who is best known for his dark and moody paintings of Iceland's landscape. Kjarval was a master of capturing Iceland's raw nature in the winter light. The majority of Kjarval's collection was left to the city of Reykjavík after his death. The other wing of the museum features various Icelandic artists, ranging from well-known modern artists to some of Iceland's best and brightest art students. The museum is one level with a coffeehouse in the middle of the two wings. The high ceilings and wall of windows by the coffeehouse make for an interesting space. A large outdoor field behind the museum sometimes serves as a spot for sculpture exhibitions. The museum is on the small size, so budget an hour to check out the art.

ÁSMUNDARSAFN

Ásmundarsafn (Sigtún, tel. 354/553-2155, www.listasafnreykjavikur.is) is an impressive sculpture museum featuring only the works of Ásmundur Sveinsson (1893-1982), who worked with materials including wood, copper, and iron. Ásmundur's work is housed in a gorgeous stark white domed building. It's small, so you only need an hour or less to explore the work, but it's an hour well spent. An exhibit features what his workshop looked like, as well as renderings of projects, and his masterpiece, a chair carved out of wood. The detail of the chair is spectacular. An outdoor sculpture garden features interesting works among trees, shrubs, and flowers.

Reykjavík's stunning setting

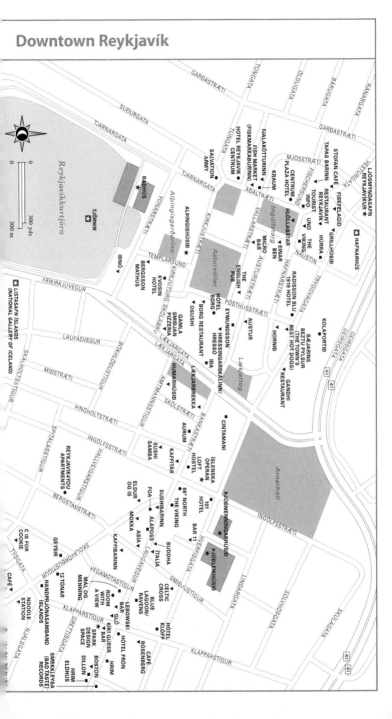

Downtown Reykjavík

Þjóðmenningarhúsið (Culture House)

Culture House (Hverfisgata 15, tel. 354/545-1400, www.thjodmenning. is, 11am-5pm daily, 1,000ISK) is a stately white neoclassic building that first opened to the public in 1909 as a museum. It is home to significant medieval manuscripts, including unique sagas, narratives, and poems from early settlers. Guided tours of exhibitions on Mondays and Fridays at 3pm last about an hour, or you can tour on your own. Rotating exhibitions throughout the year can include paintings, photography, or literary works. The exhibits do an excellent job of placing the manuscripts, literature, and artwork in context, giving visitors a great overview. Be sure to check the website to see what's on view. Culture House also plays host to conferences, gatherings, and readings throughout the year, including Reykjavík's annual design festival, DesignMarch, in the spring. The cafeteria serves light meals, and the traditional meat soup is delicious.

★ Hallgrímskirkja

Hallgrímskirkja (Hallgrímstorg, tel. 354/510-1000, www.hallgrimskirkja. is, 9am-9pm daily June-Aug., 9am-5pm daily rest of year, free) is one of the most photographed, and most visited, sites in Reykjavík. The "Church of Hallgrímur" is a national monument dedicated to Hallgrímur Pétursson, one of the most cherished and celebrated poets of Iceland, who lived 1614-1674. It's a modern structure, made out of concrete, that has basalt-style columns at the bottom coming to a point at the top.

Standing at 73 meters, the Lutheran church was designed by state architect Guðjón Samúelsson, and work started on the church in 1945. Completed in 1986, the church is a must-see for tourists. The interior is home to a gorgeous organ constructed by Johannes Klais Organworks in Germany, as well as beautiful stained-glass windows. Concerts ranging from choirs to organ performances are frequently held at the church. Be

Hallgrímskirkja

sure to check the website for upcoming concerts. An annual Christmas concert features traditional songs sung in English. It's an active church that holds services.

The highlight of a trip to Hallgrímskirkja for many is a visit to the **tower** (9am-9pm daily June-Aug., 9am-5pm daily rest of year, 800ISK) at the top, which has spectacular views of the city. An elevator takes you to the tower.

Einar Jónsson Museum

The **Einar Jónsson Museum** (Eiríksgata 1, tel. 354/561-3797, www. lej.is, 1pm-5pm daily June-mid-Sept., 1pm-5pm Sat.-Sun. mid-Sept.-Nov. and Feb.-May, closed Dec.-Jan., 1,000ISK) houses the works of one of Iceland's most celebrated sculptors, Einar Jónsson (1874-1954). Situated across the street from Hallgrímskirkja, the museum features work ranging from Christian-themed sculptures to those depicting Iceland's rich folklore. Einar worked almost entirely with plaster, which was rare for the period. The outdoor sculpture garden is beautiful, whether the sun is shining or it is under a layer of snow. The garden makes the museum a very special visit. Plan to spend about an hour checking out the art inside, and if the weather is nice, spend additional time outside in the garden.

Hið Íslenzka Reðasafn (Icelandic Phallological Museum)

The **Icelandic Phallological Museum** (Laugavegur 116, tel. 354/561-6663, www.phallus.is, 10am-6pm daily, 1,000ISK) is just as weird as it sounds. Guests can view the penises of 200 Icelandic animals, including the arctic fox, walrus, seal, and polar bear. After the museum was moved to its current location in Reykjavík (from Húsavík in North Iceland), the curator unveiled his latest acquisition—a human member. The museum has members on display in glass cases, and preserved bones of certain mammals are hanging on the wall. The highlight is also a unique photo op: the huge whale specimen on display. Some people find the museum humorous, while others are a bit freaked out. Looking for unique postcards, T-shirts, and souvenirs? Look no further.

Spark Design Space

Spark Design Space (Klapparstígur 33, tel. 354/552-2656, www.spark-designspace.com, 10am-6pm Mon.-Fri., noon-4pm Sat., free) was a welcome addition to the Reykjavík gallery scene. Before Spark opened in 2010, Reykjavík did not have a gallery dedicated to product design, which is surprising for such a design-conscious city. The gallery has rotating exhibitions ranging from poster design to home goods to 3D printer demonstrations. Spark plays a role in local events and festivals; it's a venue during Reykjavík's annual spring design festival, DesignMarch. Just off Laugavegur, the main street in downtown Reykjavík, Spark is in a great location among cool shops and popular bars.

Þjóðminjasafn Íslands (National Museum of Iceland)

The National Museum of Iceland (Suðurgata 41, tel. 354/530-2200, www. nationalmuseum.is, 10am-5pm daily May-mid-Sept., 11am-5pm Mon., 10am-5pm Tues.-Sun. mid-Sept.-Apr., 1,500ISK) is Reykjavík's main heritage and history museum, housing everything from tools and clothing of the settlement era to models of Viking-era ships. This is the best museum in the city to get insight on the history of the Icelandic nation and its people. The artifacts and exhibitions are well presented with clear information in English. Budget about two hours to take in all exhibits.

Saga Museum

The Saga Museum (Grandagardi 2, tel. 354/511-1517, www.sagamuseum. is, 10am-6pm daily, 2,000ISK) moved to its new location in 2014 after being housed in Perlan for years. With the move came a bigger and reinvigorated museum, with 17 exhibits ranging from Iceland's first inhabitants to the nation's conversion to Christianity to the reformation. Special emphasis is placed on important characters in Iceland's history, such as Ingólfur Arnarson, who is believed to be the first settler in Iceland. There are interactive displays as well as artifacts on view and even a Viking dress-up area that is great for kids. They can play with replicas of traditional clothing and plastic swords. An audio guide in English, German, French, or Swedish is available to accompany your walk around the museum. The in-house café, Kol & Salt, serves light meals, coffee, and a selection of wine and beer. The cakes are very tempting. It's best to budget two hours for this museum.

Norræna Húsið (Nordic House)

Nordic House (Sturlugata 5, tel. 354/551-7030, www.nordichouse.is, 11am-5pm Sun.-Wed., 11am-9pm Thurs.-Sat., free) is home to a library, café, and numerous cultural events during the year. For instance, literary and film festivals are held at the building, as well as fashion and music events. Most tourists visit Nordic House for the structure itself. The building, which was opened in 1968, was designed by noted Finnish architect Alvar Aalto, and several of his signature traits are reflected in the design, including the use of tile, white, and wood throughout the building. The exterior features a one-story design with a blue ceramic rooftop.

Ljósmyndasafn Reykjavíkur (Reykjavík Museum of Photography)

The Reykjavík Museum of Photography (Tryggvagata 15, tel. 354/563-1790, www.photomuseum.is, noon-7pm Mon.-Thurs., 1pm-5pm Fri.-Sun., free) has an extensive collection of photographs, as well as items and documents related to the practice of photography, from professional and amateur photographers in Iceland. The collection is divided into three categories: landscape, press, and portrait photography. The museum is small, but there are a lot of treasures to be found, including the oldest photo in the museum's collection, a landscape photo, which dates from 1870. Iceland's most famous landscape photographer, Ragnar Axelsson, regularly has photos on exhibit.

★ Listasafn Íslands (National Gallery of Iceland)

If you have time for only one art museum, the National Gallery of Iceland (Fríkirkjuvergur 7, tel. 354/515-9600, www.listasafn.is, 10am-5pm Tues.-Sun. mid-May-mid-Sept. 15, 11am-5pm Tues.-Sun. mid-Sept.-mid-May, 1,000ISK) should be it due to its large and varied collection. The National Gallery houses the country's main collection of Icelandic art, with particular emphasis on 19th- and 20th-century Icelandic and international art. Here you will see everything from traditional landscape paintings to art depicting the sagas to works by modern Icelandic artists. Works from international artists on display include some from Pablo Picasso and Richard Serra. The stately white building is a stone's throw from Tjörnin (The Pond), so if the weather is fair, taking a leisurely stroll after visiting the museum is quite nice.

Raðhús (Reykjavík City Hall)

Reykjavík's City Hall (Tjarnagata 11, tel. 354/411-1111, www.visitreykjavik.is) is more than just a building that houses the mayor and other officials. Built in 1992, the large white structure has a wall of windows overlooking the pond. On the ground floor, visitors will find an information desk with maps and tourist brochures, as well as a cozy café with a great view of the pond and city. A large hall is often used for art exhibitions and markets, and a huge model of Iceland is a favorite among tourists and is worth a visit.

★ Tjörnin

Tjörnin (The Pond) is a small body of water, rich with birdlife, situated next to the Reykjavík City Hall building. Its scenic strip of colorful houses begs to be photographed. When the weather is nice, a walk around the pond,

the National Gallery of Iceland

which is about 1.5 kilometers around, is delightful. Sculptures and benches dot the perimeter. Birdlife is plentiful, with arctic terns, ducks, seagulls, and swans. Feeding the birds is not allowed, so don't be that tourist who empties a bag of stale bread at the edge. In the winter, the pond freezes and becomes popular for ice skating.

Alþingishúsið (Parliament House)

The Alþingishúsið is the meeting place of the national parliament members of Iceland. While Iceland's democracy dates back to the year 930, and parliament members met at Þingvellir, the parliament was moved to Reykjavík in 1844. Situated near Austurvöllur park, the stone building was designed by Danish architect Ferdinand Meldahland and built in 1881. Currently, only the debating chamber and a few small meeting rooms are actually located the building. It's not possible to attend sessions of parliament. Offices of most of Alþingi's members are in other buildings in the area around Austurvöllur, which is actually the address of the building.

OLD HARBOR

Reykjavík's old harbor has been undergoing a transformation over the past few years, and it's become a dynamic place to visit, with shops, museums, new hotels, and the Ólafur Elíasson-designed Harpa concert hall.

★ Harpa

Reykjavík's newest landmark, Harpa (Austurbakki 2, tel. 354/528-5000, www.harpa.is) is a striking glass structure that hosts rock concerts, operas, the Icelandic Symphony, and international conferences. Designed by Icelandic/Danish artist Ólafur Elíasson, the concert hall's exterior features individual glass panels that light up during the darkness of winter. Individual glass panels sometimes blink in a pattern, or simply change colors. The building is particularly striking since it's so close to the water

City Hall

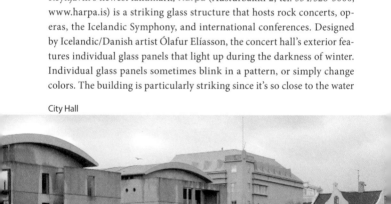

in the harbor area. Since opening its doors in 2011, Harpa has been lauded by design organizations and magazines around the world, even earning the title of "Best Performance Venue of 2011" by *Travel & Leisure* magazine. There are daily guided tours of the building available for 1,750ISK, but it's also a fun place to explore and take pictures, even if you're not going to attend a concert or conference. A café on the bottom floor serves coffee, soft drinks, light meals, and cakes, and a formal restaurant on the fourth floor has stunning views of the harbor. Two shops also occupy the first floor: the record shop 12 Tónar and the design shop Epal.

Höfði House

Höfði House (Borgartún) is one of Reykjavík's most historically significant buildings and worth a photo or two. Built in 1909, the stately white building was initially used as a consulate for France, and later served as a sort of guesthouse for famous folks passing through including Winston Churchill, the Queen of England and even actress Marlene Dietrich. Perhaps its most famous use was as the backdrop for the 1986 meeting between U.S. president Ronald Reagan and the head of the Soviet Union, Mikhail Gorbachev, that effectively ended the Cold War. Today, Höfði is owned by the City of Reykjavík and is currently used for official receptions and meetings. Although the house is unfortunately not open to the public, visitors are welcome to explore the exterior of the building.

★ Sólfar (Sun Voyager)

Situated near a coastal path popular with cyclists and runners is *Sólfar* (by the street called Sæbraut), a huge aluminum sculpture that resembles a Viking ship. Before Harpa was built, *Sólfar* was the top spot to take photos near the harbor. But, it's still a big draw for tourists and definitely worth a visit. Icelandic sculptor Jón Gunnar Árnason was inspired by undiscovered territory and chasing the sun, hence the name the *Sun Voyager*. The

Reykjavík harbor

sculpture was unveiled in 1990, just months after Jón Gunnar's death. The view of Mount Esja, the sea, and passing boats is the perfect backdrop for photos. On clear days, you can see the town of Akranes across the bay.

Aurora Reykjavík

Aurora Reykjavík (Grandagarður 2, tel. 354/780-4500, www.aurorareykjavik.is, 9am-9pm daily, 1,600ISK) gives you a chance to check out northern lights in any season. If you can't make it to Iceland in the wintertime, this is the next best thing. The multimedia exhibition gives a history of the aurora borealis, stories of northern lights from around the world, and an introduction to northern lights photography. The highlight of the center is a 13-minute film that shows some of the most majestic northern lights displays over the island.

Vikin Maritime Museum

Vikin Maritime Museum (Grandargarður 8, tel. 354/517-9400, www.maritimemuseum.is, 10am-5pm daily, 1,300ISK) is Reykjavík's main museum devoted to the city's fishing history. The main exhibitions show the progression from rowboats to modern trawlers and describe the trading vessels used, trading routes, and the construction of Reykjavík's harbor. There are daily tours of the coastal vessel *Odinn* available at 11am, 1pm, 2pm, and 3pm that last about an hour. The exhibitions cover the city's fishing history going back to the settlement to present day. The museum café has great views of the harbor and offers an outdoor eating area when the weather cooperates.

OUTSIDE THE CITY CENTER

Fjölskyldu- og Húsdýragarðinum (Reykjavík Zoo)

The Reykjavík Zoo (Laugardalur, tel. 354/575-7800, www.mu.is, 10am-6pm daily June-late Aug., 10am-5pm daily late Aug.-May, adults 750ISK, children 5-12 550ISK, children 4 and under free) is more park than zoo.

Harpa

You won't see monkeys or polar bears, but exhibits house horses, pigs, goats, sheep, and other farm animals. The main attraction is a pair of seals. It's a pleasant place to walk around and bring children, but it isn't much of a tourist destination. In other words, if you're not on a long trip with small children, you can skip the zoo and not feel bad about it. Inside is a tiny aquarium that houses mainly fish. In the summer months, you'll see Icelandic families taking a stroll, looking at the animals, and visiting a small play area for children. There isn't an official petting zoo, but it's common to see parents holding their children up to pet horses in a penned area.

Grasagardur Reykjavíkur (Reykjavík Botanical Garden)

The Reykjavík Botanical Garden (Laugardalur, tel. 354/411-8650, www.grasagardur.is, 10am-10pm daily May-Sept., 10am-3pm daily Oct.-Apr., free) is a beautiful spot tucked away in a quiet part of the city. East of downtown Reykjavík, the neighborhood is more residential. During the summer months, the garden is chock-full of bright flowers, hardy plants, peaceful ponds, and thriving birdlife. The café within the garden, Café Flora, is a little known spot among tourists. There, you will find locals sipping on coffee drinks and enjoying light meals while taking in the view from grand windows. If you're not visiting in the summer, you can skip the garden.

★ Perlan

Perlan (Öskjuhlíð, tel. 354/562-0200, www.perlan.is, free) was a unique addition to Reykjavík's skyline in 1991. The dome-shaped structure named "The Pearl" offers one of the best views of the city skyline. It houses a café that serves coffee and light meals, a souvenir shop next to the café, and an outdoor viewing platform (10am-10pm) that overlooks the city. The main attraction, however, is a rotating fine-dining restaurant on the top floor that completes a full rotation every two hours.

Reykjavík Zoo

BIKING

Reykjavík is a wonderful city to see by bicycle. That is, when the weather holds up. Over the past few years, there has been an initiative to designate more bike lanes and establish more places to lock up your bicycle along the streets. This isn't Amsterdam (perhaps the most bike-friendly city in Europe), but Reykjavík has come a long way. If you're in town and would like to rent a bike for an independent ride, or join a tour, **Reykjavík Bike Tours** (Ægisgarður 7, tel. 354/694-8956, www.icelandbike.com) will get you going. Their "Classic Reykjavík Bike Tour" covers about seven kilometers and takes a good 2.5 hours for 5,500ISK. Along the tour, you will see the University of Iceland campus, Reykjavík's Catholic cathedral, the parliament house, the old harbor, and more. Bicycle rentals start at 3,500ISK for four hours.

FISHING

If you'd like to try your hand at reeling in one of Iceland's freshest fish during the summer, you can rent equipment at Reykjavík harbor from **Rent a Rod** (tel. 354/869-2840, www.rentarod.is, 10am-6pm Mon.-Fri., 11am-5pm Sat.-Sun. June-Aug.). For 5,000ISK, you can rent a rod with wheel and line for two hours, including bait, single-use gloves, map of the harbor, and a life vest. You can catch trout, salmon, cod, pollock, and haddock. The staff could also arrange for fishing day tours out of the harbor. For sea angling tours, check out **Elding Whale Watching** (Ægisgarður 5, tel. 354/519-5000, www.whalewatching.is), which offers a tour with a "gourmet" twist, where you can cook and eat your catches on board the boat. The tour is available May-August. The tour is about three hours, departs daily from Reykjavík harbor at 11am, and costs 13,500ISK.

WHALE-WATCHING

Whale-watching is in some ways the best part of natural Reykjavík, in that you get to see a slice of nature just minutes from shore. **Elding Whale Watching** (Ægisgarður 5, tel. 354/519-5000, www.whalewatching.is) offers tours all year-round and boasts a 95 percent chance of seeing whales in the summer, and 80 percent chance in the winter. The guides are enthusiastic and the business is one of the oldest at the harbor. Tourists relish the sightings of minke and humpback whales, dolphins, porpoises, and various seabirds, including puffins and arctic terns. Make sure you dress warmly, even in the summer, as it can get quite cold on the open waters. Tours are about three hours long and cost 8,500ISK for adults and 4,250ISK for children. **Special Tours** (Ægisgarður 13, tel. 354/560-8800, www.specialtours.is) also runs year-round tours from Reykjavík harbor, with five daily departures May-August and one or two daily departures the remainder of the year. Tours are about three hours long and cost 8,500ISK per person.

BIRD-WATCHING

For bird-watchers, the "Puffin Express" tour, which leaves from Reykjavík harbor May through mid-August, is operated by **Special Tours** (tel. 354/560-8800, www.specialtours.is). The owners have been running bird-watching tours since 1996, provide binoculars on board, and have a 100 percent sighting success rate. The guides have a soft spot for the funny black and white birds with the brilliant beaks and take great pride in telling you all about them. A one-hour boat tour is 5,000ISK for adults and 2,500ISK for children.

SWIMMING

Swimming is a central part of Icelandic culture, and if you don't visit a pool or two during your stay in Iceland, you're missing out. Icelanders treat the pools as places for social gatherings. Visitors will see groups of friends and/or family in the pools and relaxing in hot tubs, chatting, laughing, and catching up. Each pool has its own character and local flavor, and some pools are more child-friendly than others, with slides and bigger areas designated for children. And, for roughly $5, it's a great way to spend a few leisurely hours. The pools listed here are recommended.

Laugardalslaug (Sundlaugavegur 30, tel. 354/411-5100, 7am-10pm Mon.-Fri., 8am-8pm Sat.-Sun., 600ISK) is the biggest pool facility in Reykjavík, and the one that gets the most tourists. The heated 50-meter outdoor pool is a big draw, along with the hot tubs, steam bath, and sauna. It's very crowded in the summer months (June-August) and can be loud because the giant water slide in the children's pool is a favorite among local kids.

Sundhöllin (Barónstígur, tel. 354/551 4059, 7am-10pm Mon.-Fri., 8am-7pm Sat.-Sun., 600ISK) is the only indoor pool in Reykjavík and popular among locals and tourists alike. The 25-meter pool was recently renovated, and the outdoor sundeck overlooking Hallgrímskirkja is a great spot to spend a couple of hours when the sun is shining. Sudhöllin also has a steam room and two hot tubs. Given its proximity to the city center, the pool gets a good amount of traffic.

Vesturbæjarlaug (Hofsvallagata 104, tel. 354/566-6879, 7am-10pm Mon.-Fri., 8am-10pm Sat.-Sun., 600ISK) is situated in a quiet neighborhood west of the city center. If you're looking to beat the crowds and experience the pool culture among locals, this is the spot. Facilities include a 25-meter pool, a few hot tubs, and a sauna.

SPAS

If you're after something more luxurious than a local swimming pool, there are a couple of spas in Reykjavík where you can relax and get treatments. Many tourists opt to spend an afternoon at the Blue Lagoon near Grindavík, and several buses depart from the bus station BSÍ (www.bsi.is). But if you want to beat the crowds, a local spa is a great option.

Laugar Spa (Sundlaugavegur 30A, tel. 354/553-0000, www.laugarspa.is,

6am-11pm Mon.-Fri., 8am-9:30pm Sat., 8am-7:30pm Sun.) is Reykjavík's largest private spa, offering an extensive menu of treatments including facials, body massage and scrub, tanning treatments, waxing and nail services, and clay wrap treatments. The spa is marketed as an "aquatic heaven," and it's as good as it sounds. The entrance to the spa is reminiscent of a cave, with the soothing sound of water drops falling from a six-meter-wide waterfall. Inside, six sauna rooms are kept at different temperatures, each with its own unique theme. The treatment rooms feature muted hues and calming music. There is a gym on-site, as well as a café serving fresh, healthy meals.

The **Soley Natura Spa** at Icelandair Hótel Reykjavík Natura (Nautholsvegur 2, tel. 354/444-4085, www.icelandairhotels.com, 10am-8pm Mon.-Fri., 10am-7pm Sat., noon-5pm Sun.) arrived on the scene in 2011. The spa has an earthy atmosphere with natural hues and lots of wood furnishings. It's Scandinavian to a T. Guests have access to a heated pool, hot tub, and sauna before and after treatments. Massage options include lymphatic massage, hot stone massage, reflexology, and pregnancy massage. Beauty treatments include waxing services, manicures and pedicures, and facials.

Entertainment and Events

NIGHTLIFE

Reykjavík may be small, but its nightlife is epic. Whether you're up for some live music, want to dance, or are interested a classic pub crawl, Reykjavík will not disappoint. The main drag, Laugavegur, is ground zero for the hottest clubs and bars in town. If you are up for dancing, Kiki Queer Bar is your spot. If you fancy a whiskey bar, Dillon is the place. If you want to catch a hot Reykjavík band performing live, Húrra is your best bet. Be prepared for it to be a late night and for your wallet to take a hit. Locals don't venture out until around midnight, and drinks are expensive. Expect to pay upwards of New York City and London prices for alcohol. For that reason, cocktail bars are scarce and beer is the favored beverage. But, for such a small city, you can't help but be impressed by the number of hot spots catering to different genres. Your biggest challenge will be narrowing down your options!

Dance Clubs

Austur (Austurstræti 7, tel. 354/568-1907, 8pm-1am Thurs., 8pm-4:30am Fri.-Sat.) was once the hottest club in Reykjavík, but a dress code and competition from other clubs have knocked Austur down a couple of pegs. It's still a place to go, mingle with locals, and dance the night away with current and trendy dance music.

Boston (Laugavegur 28B, tel. 354/577-3200, 4pm-1am Mon.-Thurs., 4pm-3am Fri.-Sat.) is best known as a hangout for local artists, writers,

Lebowski Bar

Kiki Queer Bar

hipsters, and hangers-on. The bar has an unassuming exterior, but inside await good drinks and hot music, mainly rock. If there's a concert on the night you go, expect to stand shoulder to shoulder. It's a tight spot and doesn't take too long to draw a big crowd.

Hressingarskálinn (Austurstræti 22, tel. 354/561-2240, www.hresso. is, 9am-1am Sun.-Thurs., 10am-4am Fri.-Sat.), simply known as Hresso, is a casual restaurant by day, serving up hamburgers and sandwiches. Free Wi-Fi attracts writers, tourists, and locals, who are known to spend hours sipping endless cups of coffee. By night, Hresso transforms into a dance club, with hot DJs and live bands. Expect current and trendy dance music.

Lebowski Bar (Laugavegur 20, tel. 354/552-2300, www.lebowski.is, 11:30am-1am Sun.-Thurs., 11:30am-4am Fri.-Sat.) not so subtly pays homage to the Coen brothers' movie *The Big Lebowski*. Inside there is bowling paraphernalia, posters from the film, and even a rug hanging on the side of the bar. It's a casual eatery during the day, like many of Reykjavík's bars, but at night it transforms into a pretty wild scene, playing the latest dance music. There's a dance floor in the back end of the bar.

Bars

Celtic Cross (Hverfisgata 26, tel. 354/511-3240, 11am-1am Sun.-Thurs., 11am-5am Fri.-Sat.) has Guinness on tap, which is the only thing that makes this place remotely Irish despite wood paneling and Irish ale ads on the walls. But, locals come for the Guinness and it attracts tourists as well. Crowds are known to be rowdy on the weekends.

The English Pub (Austurstræti 12b, tel. 354/578-0400, www.enskibar-inn.is, noon-1am Mon.-Fri., noon-4:30am Sat.-Sun.) is part English pub, part sports bar. There's a nice selection of Icelandic and foreign beer, and Guinness is on tap. If there's a soccer game being played anywhere in the world, it will likely be shown on one of the many screens in the bar. If there's an English league game on, expect a crowd of expats, tourists, and locals.

Kaffibarinn (Bergstaðastræti 1, tel. 354/551-1588, 5pm-1am Sun.-Thurs., 3pm-3am Fri.-Sat.) has been a Reykjavík institution since scenes from the indie film *101 Reykjavík* were filmed in the bar. Damon Albarn, the Blur frontman, used to own a stake in the bar. It's a tiny bar, with a rich red exterior, that gets jam-packed during the weekends, but it's one of those places that it's cool to say you were there. Expect trendy dance music to be blaring as you enter.

Micro Bar (Austurstræti 6, tel. 354/847-9084, 4pm-midnight daily) is a beer lover's paradise. The bar carries about 80 different beers from countries including Belgium, Germany, Denmark, and the United States. The big draws are the wide selection of Icelandic beers on tap and the number of Icelandic craft beers available. Stop by and try a local stout, pale ale, or lager. The atmosphere is relaxed and relatively quiet, with dim lighting and a large wood bar. You'll find locals at one of the tables enjoying a beer and conversation with a friend.

Gay and Lesbian

Kiki Queer Bar (Laugavegur 22, tel. 354/571-0194, www.kiki.is, 8pm-1am Thurs., 8pm-4:30am Fri.-Sat.) is Reykjavík's only gay bar and was a welcome addition to the scene when it opened its doors in early 2013. Many locals will tell you this is *the* place to go to dance because it attracts some of the best local and visiting DJs. You can expect music ranging from Madonna to Lady Gaga and everything in between.

Live Music

Bar 11 (Hverfisgata 18, tel. 354/690-6021, noon-1am Sun.-Thurs., noon-3am Fri.-Sat.) has earned its reputation as Reykjavík's leading rock bar by featuring a steady stream of up-and-coming rock bands as well as local favorites. The decor is dark, with skulls and black furnishings, but the attitude is light and fun.

Café Rósenberg (Lækjargata 2, tel. 354/551-8008, 11am-1am Sun.-Thurs., 11am-3am Fri.-Sat.) is known to host jazz, pop, rock, and folk acts from all around Iceland. You have a good chance to catch local favorites like KK, Ellen, and Svavar Knutur here, as well as international acts. The staffers are warm and friendly music lovers who take pride in booking varied acts and running a laid-back café that serves classic Icelandic comfort food.

Dillon (Laugavegur 30, tel. 354/511-2400, 2pm-1am Sun.-Thurs., 2pm-3am Fri.-Sat.) looks and feels like a dive bar. Rockers, metalheads, and hipsters unite, listening to live bands and sipping the fine collection of whiskeys available. When there isn't live music, local DJs keep the music flowing. The interior is a little rough, with lots of wood and not many places to sit, and the music is always loud.

Húrra (Tryggvagata 22, tel. 354/691-9662, 5pm-1am Sun.-Thurs., 5pm-4:30am Fri.-Sat.) is a colorful spot featuring a steady stream of Iceland's hottest bands taking the stage, playing everything from rock and dance to pop and hip hop, depending on the night.

Kex Hostel (Skulagata 28, tel. 354/561-6060, www.kexhostel.is) has become a Reykjavík institution over the past few years. The hostel, which used to be home to a biscuit factory, is a great space, complete with midcentury furniture, vintage wall maps, and a lot of curiosities. A small stage in the entryway hosts up and coming bands while guests drink and hang out at the bar. A back room serves as a concert space for more formal concerts. If you're in your 20s and aren't bothered by hipsters, this is your place. Since this is a hostel, it's open 24 hours, so check listings at www.grapevine.is for concert times.

Loft Hostel (Bankastræti 7, tel. 354/553-8140, www.lofthostel.is) opened in 2013 and has quickly earned a reputation as a place to see and be seen. The fourth-floor bar/café hosts up and coming bands, established live acts, and DJs. An outdoor deck overlooks Bankastræti and is packed with locals and tourists alike when the sun is shining during the day, and filled with mingling concertgoers at night. Since this is a hostel, it's open 24 hours, so check listings at www.grapevine.is for concert and event times.

PERFORMING ARTS

Íslenska Óperan (Icelandic Opera)

The Icelandic Opera (Ingólfsstræti 2A, tel. 354/511-6400, www.opera.is) has been thriving since productions moved in 2011 to the exquisite Harpa concert hall by the harbor. Productions have become more elaborate, and entire runs have been selling out. If you are an opera fan, check the website to see the current and upcoming shows. Past performances include *Carmen, Il Trovatore, La Boheme,* and *The Magic Flute.*

Sinfóníuhljómsveit Íslands (Icelandic Symphony Orchestra)

The Icelandic Symphony Orchestra (Austurbakki 2, tel. 354/545-2500, www.sinfonia.is) consists of 90 full-time members and performs about 60 concerts each season, including subscription concerts in Reykjavík, family concerts, school concerts, and recordings, as well as local and international tours. Based in the Harpa concert hall, the symphony has performed works by Igor Stravinsky, Sergei Rachmaninoff, and Pyotr Tchaikovsky.

Þjóðleikhúsið (National Theater of Iceland)

The National Theater of Iceland (Hverfisgata 19, tel. 354/551-1200, www.leikhusid.is) has been a Reykjavík mainstay since its opening in 1950. The emphasis is on Nordic/Scandinavian plays and musicals, but some foreign works are translated into Icelandic. For instance, in 2014, the theater put on a production of the Monty Python musical *Spamalot* in the 500-seat main stage. The exterior is a cold, concrete-gray building, but inside is a different story. The interior is modern, the theaters comfortable, and there's a lovely lounge area with plush seats and small tables where you can have a drink and wait for the show to begin.

FESTIVALS AND EVENTS

Spring

Launched in 2009, the **Reykjavík Fashion Festival** (www.rff.is) showcases fashion lines from established designers as well as up-and-comers every March for four days. Along with runway shows and special exhibitions, the festival welcomes international designers as guest speakers. In 2014, Calvin Klein was a guest.

Coinciding with the Reykjavík Fashion Festival is **DesignMarch** (www.designmarch.is), a broader event that covers everything from product design to graphic design. With pop-up stores around the city and exhibitions held in museums and open-air spaces, the festival attracts people from around the world to check out the latest and greatest in Icelandic design.

You may not expect Reykjavík to be a blues town, but don't tell that to locals. The **Reykjavík Blues Festival** (www.blues.is) is a week-long festival held in early April. It mixes local talent with acclaimed international acts like Michael Burks, Lucky Peterson, Pinetop Perkins, and Magic Slim and the Teardrops.

Gamers rejoice! The **EVE Fanfest** takes over the city every May, celebrating the beloved video game *EVE*, which is the creation of local company CCP. Thousands of gamers, nerds, and curious locals gather, attend round-table discussions, play live tournaments, and indulge in a pub crawl.

Summer

Delighting locals and tourists since 1970, the **Reykjavík Arts Festival** (www.artfest.is) manages to keep the program fresh, showcasing visual and performance artists from around the globe. The festival spans two weeks over late May/early June and holds events in different cultural venues as well as outdoor exhibitions.

Reykjavík Pride (www.reykjavikpride.com) is a citywide celebration of human rights, diversity, and culture. It garners a huge turnout every year. Each August, the city hosts rainbow-themed events ranging from concerts to guest speakers. It's known as the highest-profile event for Iceland's gay, lesbian, bisexual, and transgender community. Hundreds of volunteers organize the event, and people from around the country congregate to celebrate their fellow citizens.

Since 1990, the **Reykjavík Jazz Festival** (www.reykjavikjazz.is) has been delighting horn section enthusiasts. International artists like Aaron Parks and Chris Speed are invited to put on concerts and jam with locals over five days in mid-August. There are off-venue free events throughout the city, and this is a popular festival among the locals. Main concerts take place at the concert hall Harpa.

Independent choreographers launched the **Reykjavík Dance Festival** (www.reykjavikdancefestival.com) in 2002, and the annual event is still going strong today. The focus is on bringing contemporary dance closer to the people. The week-long event held every August showcases local talent as well as international dancers.

Reykjavík Culture Night (www.menningarnott.is) has the darling slogan "come on in," which is a reference to the old-fashioned customs of hospitality. Culture Night actually starts during the day, with select residents opening up their properties to offer waffles and coffee to their neighbors and visitors. Hundreds of events around the city range from cultural performances to free museum events. The festival culminates with a huge outdoor concert that features some of the biggest names in Icelandic rock and pop music. It's held at the end of August.

Fall

Beginning at the end of September, the Reykjavík International Film Festival (www.riff.is) takes place over 11 days, during which films from more than 40 countries are screened. They range from short films to full-length features and documentaries, and the festival is a great venue to discover new talent. Invited special guests have included American director Jim Jarmusch and English director Mike Leigh.

Iceland Airwaves (www.icelandairwaves.is) has been delighting music lovers since 1999. The five-day festival, held in late October/early November, has hosted an impressive list of performers, including Sigur Rós, Björk, and Of Monsters and Men, as well as international artists including Robyn, Kraftwerk, and Flaming Lips. There are also off-venue performances held for free in bars, bookstores, record shops, and coffeehouses—so if you don't score tickets to the festival, you can still check out some amazing music. A detailed off-venue schedule is published along with on-venue appearances.

Winter

Sónar Reykjavík (www.sonarreykjavik.com) is the new kid on the block in Reykjavík music festivals. Launched in 2013, Sónar features rock, pop, punk, electronic, and dance music performances in Harpa concert hall. Artists have included GusGus, Squarepusher, and Hermigervill. The festival takes place in middle of February.

The annual Reykjavík Food & Fun Festival (www.foodandfun.is) showcases the culinary exploits of world-renowned chefs collaborating with local Icelandic chefs. There are competitions, exhibitions, and lots of eating. It takes place at the end of February.

Shopping

Reykjavík may not strike you as a shopping destination, but there are quite a few local brands, like clothing labels 66 North and Cintamanti, that are quite popular. The high street in the city, Laugavegur, is chock-full of design shops, jewelers, boutiques, and bookstores. If you're up for some shopping, be sure to take a stroll on Laugavegur.

ART/DESIGN

Aurum (Bankstræti 4, tel. 354/551-2770, www.aurum.is, 10am-6pm Mon.-Fri., 11am-5pm Sat.-Sun.) is the place to go for unique Icelandic jewelry. Shoppers are treated to an impressive display of rings, necklaces, and earrings made from silver, gold, or lava stones. Aurum's jewelry is distinctively Icelandic, with pieces inspired by the raw nature of the island. An adjoining part of the store is dedicated to modern toys for kids, knitwear, accessories, and home goods.

Epal (Skeifan 6, tel. 354/568-7733, www.epal.is, 10am-6pm Mon.-Fri., 11am-4pm Sat., closed Sun.) is the original design store in Iceland, stocking everything from furniture to light fixtures to bedding and small goods. At Epal, which was founded in 1975, you'll find Icelandic designers as well as international brands, including Fritz Hansen, Georg Jensen, Marimekko, OK Design, and Tin Tin. Other than the main location at Skeifan, Epal has two other stores at Keflavík International Airport and Harpa concert hall.

Foa (Laugavegur 2, tel. 354/571-1433, 11am-6pm daily) is a new addition to the Laugavegur design store scene. Since opening its doors in late 2013, Foa has carried "indie" design brands that can't be found in many other stores. For instance, there are hand-carved wooden swans by local artist Bjarni Þór on sale as well as small woolen goods for kids and individual letterpress cards. It's a fun store to wander around and pick up something unique.

Hrím (Laugavegur 25, tel. 354/553-3003, www.hrim.is, 10am-6pm Mon.-Sat., 1pm-5pm Sun.) is where you go for one-stop shopping for design lovers, whether you're looking for accessories, playful paper goods, or housewares. There is an emphasis on Icelandic design, especially when it comes to jewelry and home goods, but there are also foreign-made items as well. For instance, Hrím has an impressive Lomography camera display for those looking for lo-fi film or a new Diana plastic camera. The staff is friendly and eager to help you find that perfect purchase.

Hrím Eldhus (Laugavegur 32, tel. 354/553-2002, 10am-6pm Mon.-Sat., 1pm-5pm Sun.) was opened in 2014 after the success of parent shop Hrim, down the block. Eldhus, which means kitchen in Iceland, focuses on modern design accessories for the kitchen and dining room. The adorable store stocks goods from local Icelandic designers as well as designers from its Scandinavian and Nordic neighbors. This store is stocked with nothing you really need, but everything you want.

Kraum (Aðalstræti 10, tel. 354/517-7797, www.kraum.is, 9am-6pm

Mon.-Fri., 10am-5pm Sat., noon-5pm Sun.) has been voted "the best place to stock up on local design" by local newspaper *The Reykjavík Grapevine* for five years in a row. Kraum stocks everything from the adorable independent children's clothing line As We Grow to handbags made from fish leather. They also carry pillows, jewelry, candleholders, and woolen goods. If you're going to visit one design shop in Reykjavík, it should be Kraum, as it has the largest and most diverse selection of goods.

BOOKSTORES

Reykjavík was named a UNESCO City of Literature in 2012, and the title was well deserved. Locals like to boast that 1 in 10 Icelanders will publish a book in their lifetime and that Iceland has the highest number of Nobel Prize winners for literature per capita. That would be one winner—Halldór Laxness for *Independent People*. Due to the importance of literature to the city and the exceptionally high literacy rate of citizens, Reykjavík boasts an unusually high number of bookstores.

Eymundsson (Austurstræti 18, tel. 354/540-2000, www.eymundsson.is, 10am-10pm daily) is the oldest and largest bookstore chain in Reykjavík, dating back to 1872. The main shop on Austurstræti has four levels, with an impressive magazine section, tourist books on Iceland, and a large English-language book section.

IÐA (Lækjargata 2A, tel. 354/511-5001, www.ida.is, 9am-10pm daily) has a huge souvenir section that you see upon walking through the door. There are Iceland-related books, T-shirts, postcards, stuffed toys, and keychains. Walk a little farther and you will see an impressive array of art, travel, and design books, along with classic literature in English and a fine magazine collection. The top floor is home to a café that serves excellent coffee and a nice choice of light meals.

Mál og Menning (Laugavegur 18, tel. 354/515-2500, www.malogmenning.is, 9am-10pm daily), which means "Language and Culture," is a

Hrím design store

favorite among Reykjavík locals. The three-level store sells fun tourist wares on the ground floor next to the magazine section. Upstairs is a collection of art and photography books, along with hundreds of English-language novels and nonfiction reads. The top floor also houses a café, where people sip lattes as they flip through magazines and newspapers. The bottom floor sells office and craft supplies.

MUSIC

Icelandic music is more than Björk and Sigur Rós, and a few choice music shops will help you discover local favorites as well as up-and-coming Icelandic artists.

A lot more than a record shop, 12 Tónar (Skólavörðustígur 15, tel. 354/511-5656, www.12tonar.is, 11am-6pm daily) is a place to mingle with other music lovers and sample new Icelandic music with private CD players and headphones, all while sipping on a complimentary cup of coffee. The shop was founded in 1998 and is an integral part of Reykjavík's music culture; the owner also runs an independent music label, and the shop is often used as a music venue during Reykjavík's annual autumn music festival, Iceland Airwaves.

If you like vinyl, Lucky Records (Rauðarárstígur 10, tel. 354/551-1195, www.luckyrecords.is, 9am-10pm Mon.-Fri., 11am-10pm Sat.-Sun.) is the place for you. The shop has the largest collection of new and used vinyl in the city, with an extensive Icelandic selection as well as foreign rock, pop, hip-hop, jazz, soul, and everything else you could imagine. Bands and DJs frequently play free concerts at the shop, and it's a fun place to spend a couple of hours. There's a turntable and headphones, with which you're welcome to sample used records.

Smekkleysa (Bad Taste) Records (Laugavegur 28, tel. 354/534-3730, www.smekkleysa.net, 11am-6pm daily) was born from the legendary Smekkleysa record label that has released albums from the Sugarcubes,

coffee at Mál og Menning bookshop

Sigur Rós, and scores of other Icelandic artists. Its record shop, while small, has a great collection of Icelandic music on CD and vinyl, as well as a DVD section, box sets, and classical music on CD.

CLOTHING/KNITWEAR

Perhaps Iceland's best known and oldest brand, 66 North (Bankastræti 5, tel. 354/535-6600, www.66north.com, 9am-9pm Mon.-Sat., 10am-9pm Sun.) has been keeping Icelanders warm since 1926. You will find hats, rainwear, gloves, fleece, vests, and parkas in colors ranging from basic black (a favorite among Icelanders) to lava orange. Heavy parkas cost an arm and a leg (around $500), but you pay for the Thermolite insulation and design details. If you're not looking to make a fashion investment, you can grab a hat for about $20.

Cintamani (Bankastræti 7, tel. 354/533-3390, www.cintamani.is, 9am-10pm daily) has been dressing Icelanders in colorful, fashionable designs since 1989. Ranging from base layers to outerwear, Cintamani is a bit more playful than 66 North with more prints and brighter colors. The emphasis is not just on style, but warmth as well with top-notch insulation.

Farmers & Friends (Holmasloð 2, tel. 354/552-1960, www.farmersmar-ket.is, 10am-6pm Mon.-Fri., 11am-4pm Sat.) is the flagship store of the wildly popular Farmer's Market clothing label. If you are looking for sweaters other than the traditional garb available at Handprjónasamband Íslands (Handknitting Association of Iceland), Farmer's Market offers everything from cardigans to capes in stylish colors and patterns. The label, which was launched in 2005, is focused on combining classic Nordic design elements with a modern aesthetic.

Geysir (Skólavörðustígur 16, tel. 354/519-6000, www.geysir.com, 10am-7pm Mon.-Sat., 11am-5pm Sun.) features clothes that combine beauty with the utility of Icelandic wool. Warm sweaters, cardigans, capes and blankets are on offer at the flagship Reykjavík shop, not too far from

12 Tónar music shop

Hallgrímskirkja. The clothes have a traditional look with some modern twists.

Handprjónasamband Íslands (Handknitting Association of Iceland) (Skólavörðustígur 19, tel. 354/552-1890, www.handknit.is, 9am-6pm Mon.-Fri., 9am-4pm Sat., 11am-4pm Sun.) is a collective of Icelanders that knit and sell sweaters, scarves, shawls, hats, mittens, and other woolen goods. If you are looking for an authentic, traditional Icelandic sweater, and are willing to pay top dollar, this is your place. There are a lot of colors and patterns to choose from in an array of sizes.

Kolaportið (Tryggvagata 19, tel. 354/562-5030, www.kolaportid.is, 11am-5pm Sat.-Sun.) is Reykjavík's only flea market, and, boy, do they go all out in this space. You can find everything from secondhand traditional Icelandic sweaters, to used CDs and vinyl records, to books and even fresh and frozen fish. It's a very popular place to stop by and it's usually packed, regardless of the weather or season.

KronKron (Laugavegur 63b, tel. 354/562-8388, www.kronbykronkron.com, 10am-6pm Mon.-Thurs., 10am-6:30pm Fri., 10am-5pm Sat.) is a hip shop that focuses on up and coming designers. Fashions range from fun and flirty to chic and modern. You can find elegant dresses, fashion forward sweaters and unique accessories. The clientele ranges from teens to young professionals, which shows the range of duds available.

Steinunn (Grandagarður 17, tel. 354/588-6649, www.steinunn.com, 11am-6pm Mon.-Fri., 1pm-4pm Sat., closed Sun.) is a modern, signature collection by Steinunn Sigurðardóttir that features a love of knits, detail and craft. Popular among Icelandic women, the clothes are sleek, chic and feminine, and are frequently shown during the Reykjavík Fashion Festival in the spring. The label was launched in 2000 after Steinnun cut her teeth in New York working for the likes of Calvin Klein and Ralph Lauren.

Handknitting Association of Iceland

GIFTS AND SOUVENIRS

Álafoss (Laugavegur 8, tel. 354/562-6303, www.alafoss.is, 9am-10pm daily) is best known for its huge factory wool store in the Reykjavík suburb Mosfellsbær, but this small downtown outpost is great for picking up yarn for knitting projects and small wool souvenirs to bring home. You can find socks, hats, magnets, shot glasses, soft toys, candy, and handmade Icelandic soap, among many other goodies.

Blue Lagoon (Laugavegur 15, tel. 354/420-8849, www.bluelagoon.com, 10am-6pm Mon.-Fri., 10am-4pm Sat., 1pm-5pm Sun.) is a tiny shop on the main street that carries all of the Blue Lagoon's skin-care line. If you can't make it to the actual Blue Lagoon near Grindavík, don't fret, because you can take home some of the essence that makes the site so special. The shop is decked out in cool blue hues and lots of lava stones, and the shelves are filled with everything from a nourishing algae mask to mineral bath salts.

The Little Christmas Shop (Laugavegur 8, tel. 354/552-2412, 10am-6pm Mon.-Fri., 10am-5pm Sat., 10:30am-2pm Sun.) is a small shop where it's Christmas all year-round. A pair of stone Santa shoes outside the store draws you into a world of Christmas tree ornaments, ceramic Yule Lads figurines, soft toys, dishes, and just about everything with a Christmas theme. No matter what the season, it's a joyous shop to visit and will get you buying Christmas ornaments in July.

Polar Bear Gift Store (Laugavegur 38, tel. 354/578-6020, www.isbjorninn.is, 10am-8pm daily) is bound to catch your attention due to the huge toy polar bear models outside the store. While polar bears are not indigenous to Iceland, don't let that fact stop you from checking out the cute wares inside. You can pick up T-shirts, hats, magnets, keychains, and other souvenirs. The selection of souvenirs does not focus on polar bears, but the huge stuffed polar bears outside the store tend to draw in tourists.

Ravens (Laugavegur 15, tel. 354/551-1080, www.ravens.is, 10am-7pm Mon.-Sat., 11am-5pm Sun.) is a unique shop that houses all sorts of good

The Little Christmas Shop

stuff that you can't find anywhere else. You can find arctic fur, authentic Inuit art, lambskin rugs, custom-made knives, sculptures, and leather accessories. You won't find mass-produced souvenirs here.

The Viking (Hafnarstræti 3, tel. 354/551-1250, www.theviking.is, 9am-7pm Mon.-Fri., 9am-6pm Sat.-Sun.) is exactly what you would expect from a souvenir shop in Reykjavík. T-shirts, mugs, stuffed puffins and polar bears, wool products, Viking helmets, and just about everything in between can be found here. If you're looking for unique and sophisticated trinkets, this isn't your spot. But, if you're up for fun and affordable items, you will likely find them here.

Vínberið (Laugavegur 43, tel. 354/551-2475, 9am-6pm Mon.-Fri., 10am-6pm Sat., noon-5pm Sun.) is a sweets shop stocked with everything from chocolates to rhubarb toffee. There's a good mix of local and foreign brands, and it would be almost impossible to not find something you like. Gift options include treats wrapped in pretty packaging. In the back there are spices and baking products, and in the summer there is frequently a mini outdoor fruit market just outside the shop. One sweet that is wildly popular among Icelanders is black licorice. You can find a selection of licorice candies with or without a chocolate coating.

SHOPPING MALLS

Kringlan (Kringlunni 4-12, tel. 354/568-9200, www.kringlan.is, 10am-6:30pm Mon.-Wed., 10am-9pm Thurs., 10am-7pm Fri., 10am-5pm Sat.-Sun.), which is a short bus ride from downtown Reykjavík, resembles just about any mall in America. There are clothing stores, a bank, a movie theater, and a food court packed with teenagers and shoppers. If the weather is particularly bad and you want to get some shopping done, it's a good destination. There's a 66 North shop in Kringlan, as well as some other Icelandic brands. Kringlan is a five-minute drive east from downtown Reykjavík, and it can be reached by Strætó bus numbers 1, 2, 3, 4, 6, 13, and 14. One-way bus fare is 350ISK, and it takes about 10 minutes from downtown Reykjavík.

Smáralind (Hagasmári 1, tel. 354/528-8000, www.smaralind.is, 11am-7pm Mon.-Thurs., 11am-9pm Fri., 11am-6pm Sat., 1pm-6pm Sun.) is located in the Reykjavík suburb Kópavogur and is one of the main shopping centers in the region for locals. You will find everything from Adidas sneakers to Levi's, but for double the price than back home. However, it offers a movie theater and an entertainment area with rides for kids if that strikes your fancy.

Accommodations in Reykjavík fall into three categories: hotels, guest-houses, and self-catering apartments. The city isn't known for luxurious hotels, but there are a few "upmarket" choices; however, they remain "no-frills" when compared to other cities in Europe. By and large, expect to pay a lot during the high season (June-August). While most of the options are downtown, there are a few outside the 101 postal code. However, given how small Reykjavík is, most options are within walking distance or are within a short bus ride to downtown.

HOTELS
Under 25,000ISK

Fosshótel Baron (Baronsstígur 2-4, tel. 354/562-3204, www.fosshotel.is, rooms from 21,000ISK) may not be pretty from the exterior, but it's clean, convenient, and in a good location in downtown Reykjavík. The 120 rooms range from standard singles and doubles to apartment-style accommodations that have kitchenettes and mini refrigerators. The lobby looks a little depressing, but the accommodating staff and the location make up for it. Guests have access to free Wi-Fi, free and plentiful parking, and an adequate included breakfast.

★ **Hótel Frón** (Laugavegur 22A, tel. 354/511-4666, www.hotelfron.is, rooms from 20,000ISK) couldn't have picked a better location if they tried. Located on the high street Laugavegur, the hotel has single, double, and apartment-style studios that are clean, bright, and comfortable. The apartments come with a small kitchen, and a couple of them feature Jacuzzi bathtubs. The downside, however, is the proximity to bars on Laugavegur, which means it can be quite noisy on Friday and Saturday nights.

Hótel Klöpp (Klapparstígur 26, tel. 354/595-8520, www.centerhotels.is, rooms from 17,000ISK) offers fresh rooms on a quiet corner in city center. Some rooms feature warm, bright hues including red walls, while others are stark white, clean, and cool. All rooms have hardwood floors and small private bathrooms. Guests have access to free Wi-Fi, assistance with booking tours is provided, and the friendly staff even offers a northern lights wake-up service in the winter when the aurora borealis is visible.

Reykjavík Lights Hotel (Suðurlandsbraut 16, tel. 354/513-9000, www.keahotels.is, rooms from 18,000ISK) is a concept design hotel with 105 rooms, including singles, doubles, triples, and group rooms. Just past the reception area is an airy lobby that houses a bar and the common eating area. Rooms are large, featuring Nordic-style decor and luxurious beds. The bathrooms are modern and stark white with showers. Located outside of city center, it's about a 10-minute walk to downtown.

Radisson Blu Saga Hotel (Hagatorg, tel. 354/525-9900, www.radissonblu.com, rooms from 22,000ISK) has a dynamite location in city center, close to the Reykjavík Art Museum and Iceland's infamous Bæjarins Beztu Plysur hot dog stand. Rooms are larger than average, many with a maritime theme that's charming. Beds are lush, and the 209 rooms are stocked with bath products from Anne Semonin. Amenities include free Wi-Fi, access to the spa and health center, and two in-house restaurants: Grillið for fine dining and Restaurant Skrudur for more casual meals.

Icelandair Hótel Reykjavík Natura (Hlídarfótur, tel. 354/444-4500, www.icelandairhotels.com, rooms from 19,500ISK) underwent a renovation in 2012, transforming itself from what was just the hotel near the domestic city airport to a hotel with a fantastic spa and eclectic restaurant. It pays homage to Reykjavík's rich art culture with murals and sculptures throughout the building. Built in 1964, the hotel has been a favorite among business travelers due to its proximity to the airport, conference facilities, and indoor swimming pool. The in-house restaurant Satt offers a delicious breakfast buffet and meals throughout the day. The main attractions, for many, are the indoor pool and Soley Natura Spa, where guests can get massages, manicures, pedicures and facial treatments. The hotel is a 20-minute walk to downtown Reykjavík, but guests are given free passes for the city bus, which stops just outside the hotel.

Over 25,000ISK

Centrum Plaza Hotel (Aðalstræti 4, tel. 354/595-8500, www.centerhotels. is, rooms from 28,000ISK) is in the heart of Reykjavík. Many of the 180 rooms have spectacular views of the city, but with that comes quite a bit of noise during the weekends. The rooms are cozy and sparsely decorated but clean and bright. The bathrooms are small, with a shower, and each room has a flat-screen TV and free Wi-Fi. The clientele is a mix of business and leisure travelers. A lounge downstairs tends to be sleepy because of the proximity of popular bars downtown.

Award-winning boutique hotel 101 Hotel (Hverfisgata 10, tel. 354/580-0101, www.101hotel.is, rooms from 58,000ISK) is quite posh for Reykjavík. Indeed, the World Travel Awards named 101 Hotel the top boutique hotel in Iceland. Rooms are modern and chic with a black-and-white color palette, wood floors, and in-room fireplaces. It's cozy and stylish at the same time. And while the rooms are pricey, the amenities are pretty great. Each room has a large walk-in shower, flat-screen TV with satellite channels, free high-speed Wi-Fi, a CD/DVD player with a Bose iPod sound dock, and bathrobes and slippers. The restaurant offers an eclectic menu with creations ranging from mussels and pomme frites to Icelandic cod with saffron risotto.

Grand Hotel Reykjavík (Sigtún 38, tel. 354/514-8000, www.grand.is, rooms from 30,000ISK) is a huge 311-room high-rise hotel just a few minutes from downtown Reykjavík. This is a favorite among business travelers and conference attendees because the hotel has meeting rooms and conference facilities. The rooms are large, with hardwood floors and comfortable yet uninspiring furnishings. The restaurant is pricey; dishes range from lamb filets with mushrooms to duck breast with parsnip.

Hilton Reykjavík Nordica (Suðurlandsbraut 2, tel. 354/444-5000, www. hiltonreykjavik.com, rooms from 36,000ISK) is a 252-room four-star hotel situated in the financial district, about a 10-minute walk to downtown Reykjavík. It attracts business travelers as well as families and individuals thanks to its comfortable rooms, top-notch service, luxurious spa, and memorable in-house restaurant, Vox. If it's not important to be in the thick of downtown Reykjavík, Hilton Reykjavík is a good option.

Hlemmur Square (Laugavegur 25, tel. 354/415-1600, www.hlemmursquare.com, rooms from 38,000ISK) bills itself as an upmarket hostel. As the name suggests, the hotel is right next to Hlemmur bus station, which is downtown's most extensive bus station, providing bus transfers to just about every part of the city. Other than being in a killer location, Hlemmur Square has a popular lounge that attracts not just hotel guests, but locals. This is a great spot for 20-somethings to meet fellow travelers and socialize.

★ **Hótel Borg** (Pósthússtræti 9-11, tel. 354/551-1440, www.hotelborg.is, rooms from 40,500ISK) is a popular choice for celebrities and politicians passing through Reykjavík. Why? Built in 1930, the 56-room four-star downtown Reykjavík hotel is elegant, modern, and steeped with old-time charm. Hotel Borg's rooms have custom-made furniture, flat-screen satellite TV, and very comfortable beds. The in-house restaurant Silfur is a favorite, and a café/bar serves light meals.

Hotel Holt (Bergstaðastæti 37, tel. 354/552-5700, www.holt.is, rooms from 40,500ISK) offers spacious, tastefully decorated rooms, some with a balcony. Holt is one of the few hotels in downtown Reykjavík that offer room service, and its service and amenities are comparable to upscale hotels in large European cities. Guests also have free access to Iceland's largest health club (World Class Fitness), free parking, free Wi-Fi, and a staff eager to assist with tour bookings and recommendations for sights and restaurants.

★ **Icelandair Hótel Reykjavík Marina** (Myrargata 2, tel. 354/560-8000, www.icelandairhotels.com, rooms from 38,000ISK) opened its doors in 2012, and the hotel is in a great location by the harbor district, close to the

Hótel Borg

whale-watching tours, restaurants, and museums. One of the most design conscious of the Icelandair Hótels chain, Reykjavík Marina features art throughout the lobby, restaurant, and rooms. You can see everything from murals by local Icelandic artists to impressive wood sculptures. The rooms are minimalist and modern, the staff warm, and the hotel is home to one of the hippest hotel bars in the city, Slipp Bar.

Kvosin Hotel (Kirkutorg 4, tel. 354/571-4460, www.kvosinhotel.is, rooms from 43,000ISK) is a gorgeous modern boutique hotel situated close to the pond and parliament in downtown Reykjavík. Rooms come in four adorably described sizes: normal, bigger, biggest, and larger than life. All rooms feature mini refrigerators, a Nespresso machine, Samsung Smart TV, and skin-care amenities from Aveda. The rooms are sleek and Scandinavian cool with accents from local Icelandic designers. Breakfast is included and served downstairs at the Bergsson restaurant, which is known for its delicious breakfast and brunch options.

Radisson Blu 1919 Hotel (Posthússtræti 2, tel. 354/599-1000, www.radissonblu.com, rooms from 38,000ISK) is an 88-room hotel that occupies a central location in the capital. Built in 1919, the hotel has undergone a couple of renovations, but it has maintained a lot of its charm. The rooms are large, with hardwood floors, sizable bathrooms, comfortable beds, and free high-speed Wi-Fi. Guests who reserve a suite are treated to a king-size bed, Jacuzzi bathtub, and bathrobe with slippers. Guests also have access to a fitness center with some basic machines. The in-house restaurant is dynamite, with a menu ranging from fresh fish caught off of Iceland's shores to lamb filets and duck breast entrées.

GUESTHOUSES
Under 25,000ISK

Reykjavík Hostel Village (Flókagata 1, tel. 354/552-1155, www.hostelvillage.is, rooms from 15,000ISK) offers rooms in five different residential houses. Rooms include dorm accommodations, singles, doubles, triples, and apartment-style studios. The decor is simple, with neutral colors and wood furnishings. It's a five-minute walk to Laugavegur, the main drag, and the prices are reasonable, making this a great option for budget travelers.

★ **Loft Hostel** (Bankastræti 7, tel. 354/553-8140, www.lofthostel.is, beds from 20,000ISK) opened in 2013 and has quickly earned a reputation as a place to be and be seen. The rooms range from dorm accommodation to privates, but the big draw is the fourth floor bar/café that hosts up-and-coming bands, established live acts, and DJs. An outdoor deck overlooks Bankastræti in downtown Reykjavík, and it is packed with locals and tourists alike when the sun is shining.

Sunna Guesthouse (Thórsgata 26, tel. 354/511-5570, www.sunna.is, rooms from 19,000ISK) offers several types of accommodations: one- and two-bedroom apartments, studios, rooms with private bathrooms, and rooms with shared bathroom facilities. All rooms are decorated in a light, minimalist style with muted colors and wood furniture. The location is key, as it's right across the street from Hallgrímskirkja in downtown Reykjavík. Guests have access to a shared kitchen to prepare meals, and a breakfast buffet is included in the price. The breakfast accommodates vegetarians as well as those with gluten allergies.

Salvation Army (Kirkjustræti 2, tel. 354/561-3203, www.guesthouse.is, rooms from 14,000ISK) is only open to tourists during the summer months because it serves as a dorm for university students between September and May. But when it's open, it's a great budget option for travelers. There are private rooms as well as dorms available in the heart of Reykjavík. Rooms and common areas are clean and convenient. Please keep in mind that because the facilities are so well-managed and in a killer location, the hostel tends to sell out for the summer, so if you're interested, book early.

Over 25,000ISK

The Adam Hotel (Skólavörðustígur 42, tel. 354/896-024, www.adam.is, rooms from 25,000ISK) underwent a significant face-lift, and each room now has a private bathroom. Rooms are small and no-frills, but the location is terrific, with several rooms overlooking Hallgrímskirkja in downtown Reykjavík. Guests tend to be young, and the hotel is a great spot to meet fellow travelers. All rooms have free Wi-Fi.

★ Kex Hostel (Skulagata 28, tel. 354/561-6060, www.kexhostel.is, rooms from 28,000ISK) is a lot more than a hostel; it's ground zero for music lovers, hipsters, and the beautiful people of downtown Reykjavík to congregate, meet for drinks, and listen to live music. The hostel offers rooms ranging from private rooms to dorm accommodations, all with shared bathroom facilities. But, most people don't stay for the style or comfort of the rooms, but for the experience Kex has to offer. The front lounge houses vintage wall maps, vintage midcentury furniture, and a small stage for live bands to plug in and play. The back room is a converted gym that hosts concerts, fashion and vinyl markets, and even food festivals. Staying at Kex means you're staying for the atmosphere, the experience.

APARTMENTS
Under 25,000ISK

Bolholt Apartments (Bolholt 6, tel. 354/517-4050, www.stay.is, rooms from 15,000ISK) offers comfortable, simple rooms just a 10-minute walk from downtown Reykjavík, which makes this well-managed apartment complex very popular. Guests have private bathrooms, small kitchenettes, and access to free Wi-Fi and free parking. A common lounge has a pool table and a couple of sofas great for unwinding and meeting fellow travelers. Bolholt is a great option for independent, budget travelers.

Einholt Apartments (Einholt 2, tel. 354/517-4050, www.stay.is, rooms from 15,000ISK) has stylish, minimalist apartments with private bathrooms and kitchenettes. Its clientele ranges from more mature travelers to 20-something backpackers. Einholt is a great downtown spot for the independent traveler to spend a couple of nights or a longer stay to get to know Reykjavík.

The options at **Reykjavík4You Apartments** (Laugavegur 85, www.reykjavik4you.com, rooms from 25,000ISK) are great spaces in a central location. Studios and one- and two-bedroom apartments are available, and all are stocked with well-equipped kitchens, spacious bathrooms, and bright decor. Apartments are clean and comfortable, with lots of light in the summer months.

Room with a View (Laugavegur 18, tel. 354/552-7262, www.roomwith-aview.is, rooms from 20,000ISK) is right next to the popular bookstore Mál og Menning and near all the great bars downtown. Rooms range from small singles to three-bedroom apartments for groups. Rooms are clean and modern, some with private bathroom facilities. Guests have access to two hot tubs as well as a common kitchen area. Be advised that because of the proximity of bars and restaurants, it can be quite noisy on Friday and Saturday nights. If you're looking for a quiet room on a sleepy street, this isn't it.

Food

Reykjavík's culinary charm may be surprising to some. While there are traditional Icelandic restaurants serving up fresh fish and tender lamb filets, there are also fantastic eateries specializing in food you may not expect to see in Iceland. For instance, there's an impressive collection of Asian and Mediterranean restaurants, which have authentic menus that incorporate the great ingredients found in Iceland. If you're in the mood for tapas, there's a place to have an exquisite meal. Craving sushi? You will not be disappointed. As for Icelandic cuisine, there are upmarket restaurants catering to foodies as well as fast food joints offering quick, affordable bites.

ASIAN

Asía (Laugavegur 10, tel. 354/562-6210, www.asia.is, 11am-11pm daily, 1,500ISK) doesn't strive to be authentic and is comparable to American-style Chinese food. The outside is a bit tacky, with sketched palm trees and a yellow painted exterior, and the inside isn't much better with knickknacks and a kitschy style. The food, however, is fine and the prices are reasonable. The menu consists of shrimp, chicken, beef, and lamb options, and a few specials are offered.

Bambus (Borgartún 16, tel. 354/517-0123, www.bambusrestaurant.is, 11:30am-11pm Mon.-Fri., 5pm-10pm Sat.-Sun., 1,750ISK) is a delightful Asian fusion restaurant mixing Thai, Japanese, and Indian influences. You will find dishes incorporating everything from curry to teriyaki and coconut milk. A salad with chicken, sweet chili, and mango is spectacular. The restaurant is decorated in a minimalist Asian-influenced style.

Buddha Café (Laugavegur 3, tel. 354/571-5522, www.buddha.is,

4:30pm-10pm Mon., 11:45am-10pm Tues.-Thurs., 11:45am-11pm Fri.-Sat., closed Sun., 2,300ISK) combines Japanese and Chinese flavors to create unique and memorable dishes. The sushi menu has mainstays like California and avocado rolls, but some of the more adventurous rolls are divine, including shrimp tempura with coriander sweet chili sauce. Main courses range from fresh fish to wok-fried beef in oyster sauce. During the week, a three-course lunch special is a steal for under 2,000ISK.

Gandhi Restaurant (Posthusstræti 17, tel. 354/511-1691, www.gandhi.is, 5:30pm-10pm daily, 3,000ISK) features the creations of two chefs from southwest India. Combining local Icelandic ingredients with traditional Indian spices, the menu offers authentic dishes like chicken vindaloo and fish masala as well as vegetarian options. The food is fresh and perfectly spiced. The butter chicken is gorgeous, rivaling that of top Indian restaurants you'd find in London.

Krua Thai (Tryggvagata 14, tel. 354/561-0039, www.kruathai.is, 11:30am-9:30pm Mon.-Fri., noon-9:30pm Sat., 5pm-9:30pm Sun., 1,500ISK) has all your favorite Thai classics, ranging from chicken pad thai to spring rolls and noodle soups. During weekdays, the restaurant has a three-course lunch special for just 1,400ISK.

Noodle Station (Skólavörðustígur 21, tel. 354/551-3199, charin_79@hotmail.com, 11am-11pm daily, 1,100ISK) is a popular spot for Reykjavík natives, students, and tourists. People flock to the tiny shop for one of the tastiest and cheapest meals you can find in downtown Reykjavík. Noodle soup is available with chicken or beef or as a vegetarian option. The smell of spices wafting down Skólavörðustígur will draw you in.

Osushi (Pósthússtræti 13, tel. 354/561-0562, www.osushi.is, 11:30am-10pm Mon.-Thurs., 11:30am-11pm Fri.-Sat., 3pm-10pm Sun., bites from 300-500ISK) is a sushi train with bites snaking their way around. Diners are treated to everything from deep-fried shrimp tempura rolls to tuna sashimi and grilled eel bites. For kids, there are chicken teriyaki kebabs, spring rolls, and even a chocolate mousse for dessert.

Ramen Momo (Tryggvagata 16, tel. 354/571-0646, www.ramenmomo.is, 11:30am-9pm Mon.-Sat., noon-5pm Sun., 1,200ISK) is an adorable hidden restaurant not too far from the harbor. Owned and operated by a Tibetan immigrant, Ramen Momo serves up glorious chicken, beef, or vegetarian ramen soup and dumplings. The nondescript eatery has an authentic feel to it, and your taste buds will thank you.

Sushibarinn (Laugavegur 2, tel. 354/552-4444, www.sushibarinn.is, 11:30am-10pm Mon.-Sat., 5pm-10pm Sun., rolls from 1,400ISK) has not only sushi roll staples like California, volcano, and shrimp tempura rolls, but also some creative combinations, including the Rice Against the Machine roll, which has salmon, cream cheese, red onions, and chili. For those who are inclined, whale sushi is on the menu as well.

Sushi Samba (Þingholtsstræti 5, tel. 354/568-6600, www.sushisamba.is, 5pm-11pm Sun.-Thurs., 5pm-midnight Fri.-Sat., rolls from 2,500ISK) combines Japanese and South American elements to create inventive and delicious sushi rolls and entrées. You'll find traditional fresh seafood like tuna, salmon, crab, lobster, and shrimp, along with South American influences like spicy salsa, jalapeño mayo, and chimichurri. Main entrées include baked vanilla-infused cod and grilled beef tenderloin with mushroom sauce, jalapeño, and coriander.

ICELANDIC

Bergsson Mathús (Templarasund 3, tel. 354/571-1822, www.bergsson.is, 7am-9pm Mon.-Fri., 7am-5pm Sat.-Sun., 1,400ISK) is known for its fantastic brunch menu and light, flavorful dishes. Try the roast beef on a bed of salad or the spinach lasagna. The eatery is also a popular coffee spot for locals.

★ **Borg Restaurant** (Póshússtræti 9, tel. 354/578-2020, www.borgrestaurant.is, 7am-1am daily, 4,000ISK) has been a fixture on the Reykjavík foodie scene for years. Located on the ground floor of Hótel Borg, the restaurant is owned and operated by world-renowned chef Völundur Völundarson, who has been featured on cooking shows around the world. The cuisine is fresh and the food local, with fish dishes ranging from blue ling to salmon and plaice. A tasting menu features the chef's choice of nine courses.

Einar Ben (Veltusundi 1, tel. 354/511-5090, www.einarben.is, 5:30pm-10pm Mon.-Fri., 5pm-10pm Sat.-Sun., 4,000ISK) is named after the Icelandic literary hero Einar Benediktsson, but tourists don't flock to the restaurant for that reason. The cozy atmosphere, friendly staff, and stellar location in city center, along with fresh fish and local lamb, make this a winner among tourists. It accommodates large groups.

Fjalakötturinn (Aðalstræti 16, tel. 354/514-6060, www.fjalakotturinn. is, lunch 11:30 am-2pm daily, dinner 6pm-10:30pm Sun.-Thurs., 6pm-11pm Fri.-Sat., 3,800ISK) is housed inside Hotel Centrum in downtown Reykjavík, but it's not only a popular place for hotel guests to visit. The inventive food, modern decor, intimate tables, and gorgeous pictures of Iceland's landscape make this spot a winner. Fresh fish including salmon, trout, catfish, and lobster is on the menu, as well as rack of lamb.

Iðnó (Vonarstræti 3, tel. 354/562-9700, www.idno.is, noon-10pm daily, entrées from 7,000ISK) is a historic building that currently houses local theater productions as well as a fine restaurant. Situated close to Tjörnin and City Hall, the restaurant is pricey, but the food is memorable. The smoked salmon on blinis with caviar is exquisite, as is the ginger-glazed breast of duck. The restaurant is often used to host private parties and family gatherings in a huge banquet room.

★ **Lækjarbrekka** (Bankastræti 2, tel. 354/551-4430, www.laekjarbrekka.is, 11:30am-10pm daily, entrées from 3,000ISK) occupies a historic building that has undergone quite a few transformations since it was built in 1834, including a bakery. Today, Lækjarbrekka is one of the best-known downtown restaurants catering to tourists. Fresh fish dishes are on the menu as well as some of Iceland's most adventurous cuisine. You'll find fermented shark, whale meat, puffin, and Icelandic horse filets on offer. For tamer choices, the pan-fried filet of lamb and arctic char are splendid.

Perlan (Öskjuhlíð, tel. 354/562-0200, www.perlan.is, 10am-11pm daily, mains from 4,200ISK) occupies the top floor of the architecturally significant building, providing breathtaking views of the city. If you are in town on New Year's Eve, this is a great place to have a late dinner. The food is classic, with fresh ingredients and nothing too outrageous. There is whale meat on the menu, but most people opt for the fresh rainbow trout or the glorious cod with rye bread and potatoes, a traditional, hearty Icelandic meal.

Restaurant Reykjavík (Vesturgata 2, tel. 354/552-3030, www.restaurantreykjavik.is, 6pm-10pm daily, mains from 4,000ISK) is known for its fantastic fish buffet, which starts every day at 6pm. This is a favorite among tourists looking to sample traditional Icelandic fish dishes as well as international classics. The restaurant is housed in a huge yellow building with lots of tables, so you're not likely to have to wait for a table. The fish buffet features everything from salmon, cod, lobster, fish balls, trout, and caviar to shrimp and crab specialties. An à la carte menu offers beef, lamb, fish, and vegetarian options.

MEDITERRANEAN

Gamla Smiðjan Pizzeria (Lækjargata 8, tel. 354/578-8555, www.gamlasmidjan.is, 11:30am-10pm daily, 1,500ISK) is a wildly popular pizza place among the locals, which is telling. While Reykjavík isn't known for its pizza, this place is pretty darn good. You have a choice of an obscene number of toppings, ranging from classic pepperoni to more exotic options like tuna fish and banana. It has a laid-back atmosphere and decent service.

Hornið (Hafnartsræti 15, tel. 354/551-3340, www.hornid.is, 11am-11:30pm daily, large pizzas from 1,790ISK) looks like a bistro from the outside with yellow and blue walls, and the interior reveals a relaxed atmosphere with friendly service and yummy pizzas. Classic pizzas include pepperoni, four cheese, and vegetable, but there are also adventurous creations like the Pizza Pecatore, which has shrimp, mussels, and scallops on top. If you're not up for pizza, entrées include salted cod with risotto and filet of lamb with vegetables.

Ítalía (Laugavegur 11, tel. 354/552-4630, www.italia.is, 11:30am-11:30pm daily, pasta dishes from 2,400ISK) is a cute Italian restaurant right on the main street, Laugavegur. The owners boast a menu that offers classics like spaghetti Bolognese, lasagna, and mushroom ravioli as well as options that incorporate local ingredients, like smoked salmon with toasted bread and pan-fried salted cod with onions. Pizza and calzone are also on the menu.

Tapas Barinn (Vesturgata 3b, tel. 354/551-2344, www.tapas.is, 5pm-11:30pm Sun.-Thurs., 5pm-1am Fri.-Sat., 3,500ISK) was a welcome addition to the Reykjavík restaurant scene. There are so many delightful choices, but if you'd like a taste of the chef's best Icelandic dishes, go for the "gourmet feast" where the chef prepares dishes with smoked puffin, Icelandic sea trout, lobster tails, grilled Icelandic lamb, minke whale with cranberry sauce, and pan-fried blue ling with lobster sauce. The seven plates, along with a shot of the famous Icelandic spirit Brennivin and a chocolate *skyr* mousse dessert will only set you back 6,690ISK. If you would like more traditional tapas, there are lots of options, including salmon and bacon-wrapped scallop bites.

Uno (Hafnarstræti 1, tel. 354/561-3131, www.uno.is, 11:30am-11pm Sun.-Thurs., 11:30am-midnight Fri.-Sat., mains from 2,800ISK) is an elegant Italian restaurant that has a lovely terrace out front where locals and tourists are seen sipping coffees and cocktails when the sun is shining. The interior is very cozy, with leather armchairs in the lounge and warm hues and artwork decorating the walls. The menu makes it hard to decide with so many tasty options. You could go traditional with chicken rigatoni or try something more exotic, like black linguine with mussels, scallops, and olives.

SEAFOOD

★ Fish Market (Aðlstræti 12, tel. 354/578-8877, www.fiskmarkadurinn.is, 6pm-11:30pm daily, mains from 4,300ISK) stands out among a number of fantastic seafood restaurants in Reykjavík. What makes Fish Market special is the combination of ingredients the chef employs. For instance, the grilled monkfish comes with crispy bacon, cottage cheese, tomato yuzu pesto, and crunchy enoki mushrooms. It's a vision, as is the salted cod with lime zest with potato puree, dried cranberries, and celery salad.

Fiskfelagid (Fish Company) (Vesturgata 2a, tel. 354/552-5300, www.fiskfelagid.is, 5:30pm-midnight daily, entrées from 3,800ISK) has a striking, chic interior with modern wooden tables and chairs, candleholders throughout the space, and personal notes and photos adorning the walls. There are comfortable couches in the lounge, where you're welcome to sip a cocktail while waiting for a table. The food is flawless, ranging from pan-fried prime lamb and oxtail with artichoke puree to blackened monkfish and fried langoustine with lobster spring rolls.

Humarhúsið (Amtmannsstígur 1, tel. 354/561-3303, www.humarhusid.is, 11am-10pm Mon.-Sat., 5pm-10pm Sun., mains from 4,400ISK) or "The Lobster House" is the place for—you guessed it—lobster. You can't make a bad choice: grilled lobster tails with garlic butter, lobster soup, slow cooked monkfish and smoked lobster with potato salad, lobster tempura, and lots of other options. If you're not a fan of lobster, don't fret. There are lamb, pork, and other fish options on the menu.

Icelandic Fish & Chips (Tryggvagata 11, tel. 354/551-1118, www.fishandchips.is, noon-9pm daily, mains from 1,290ISK) serves up a wonderful range of fresh seafood: cod, plaice, blue ling, haddock, red fish, wolf fish, and shellfish. For an authentic Icelandic fish-and-chips meal, go for the cod. The biggest draws, however, are the "skyronnaise dips," in which Iceland's famous soft cheese, *skyr,* is blended with an array of spices, including basil, coriander, ginger, and tarragon. The truffle and tarragon dip is heavenly.

the Sea Baron restaurant

Kaffitár coffee shop

MAR Restaurant (Geirsgata 9, tel. 354/519-5050, www.marrestaurant.com, 11:30am-11pm daily, mains from 3,900ISK) offers South American-inspired dishes ranging from prosciutto-wrapped monkfish with fennel seeds to lamb filet with leeks, carrots, and beets. The banana crème brûlée with chocolate sorbet is recommended for dessert. The atmosphere is casual, with wood tables and minimalist design, and its harbor location is great.

★ **Sægreifinn (Sea Baron)** (Geirsgata 8, tel. 354/553-1500, www.saegreifinn.is, 11:30am-10pm daily, mains from 1,200ISK) has been a Reykjavík institution for years. With its prime location by the harbor, the Sea Baron is known for its perfectly spiced, fresh lobster soup, which comes with a side of bread and butter. Fish kebabs on offer include scallops, monkfish, and cod. There is also whale meat available if you're inclined. Inside, visitors will find a hut-like atmosphere with fishing relics, photos, and equipment. There's a net hanging from the ceiling, and there are charming knickknacks displayed lovingly by the 90-year-old owner.

STEAKHOUSES

Argentina (Barónsstígur 11A, tel. 354/551-9555, www.argentina.is, 6pm-midnight Sun.-Thurs., 5:30pm-1am Fri.-Sat., mains from 3,900ISK) is warm and inviting the second you step through the door, with leather couches, a roaring fireplace, and the smell of choice cuts of meat wafting through the air. You can choose from rib eye, T-bone, slow-cooked ox flank, beef rump, porterhouse, and peppered beef tenderloin, among other cuts. Chicken, lamb, and seafood round out the menu, as well as an excellent wine list.

Steikhúsið (Tryggvagata 4, tel. 354/561-1111, www.steik.is, 5pm-10pm Sun.-Wed., 5pm-11pm Thurs.-Sat., steaks from 3,650ISK) opened in 2012, but it has already made a big impact on Reykjavík's restaurant scene. Guests can choose from beef rib eye, porterhouse, and T-bone cuts or lamb filets, with tasty sauces including béarnaise, creamy pepper, and blue cheese.

There are also fish entrées on offer as well as a dynamite hamburger with brie, pickled vegetables, mango chutney, chipotle, and bacon. For the adventurous, the surf-and-turf features minke whale and horse meat grilled in a coal oven.

FAST FOOD

★ **Bæjarins Beztu Pylsur (The Town's Best Hot Dog)** (Tryggvatagata 1, tel. 354/511-1566, www.bbp.is, 11:30am-12:30am Sun.-Thurs., 11:30am-4am Fri.-Sat., 380ISK) is a place that you have to visit. Even if you don't eat hot dogs, you should get a look at the tiny shack that has been delighting tourists, locals, food critics, and even U.S. president Bill Clinton for years. Located close to the harbor, the hot dog stand serves up lamb meat hot dogs, with fresh buns and an array of toppings. If you're out for a late-night bar crawl and get hungry, keep in mind that the stand is open until 4am on the weekend.

Grillhúsið (Tryggvagata 20, tel. 354/562-3456, www.grillhusid.is, 11:30am-10pm Sun.-Thurs., 11:30am-11pm Fri.-Sat., 1,500ISK) is part diner, part TGI Friday's, with Americana displayed on the walls and an extensive menu ranging from hamburgers to fish-and-chips to salads and sandwiches. They have an interesting array of burgers on offer, and the lamb/béarnaise burger is a personal favorite.

Hamborgara Búllan (Geirsgata 1, tel. 354/511-888, www.bullan.is, 11:30am-9pm daily, burgers from 730ISK) is a corner burger joint situated in the old harbor district, close to where the whale-watching tours depart. The food is tasty, the service quick, and the decor a little kitschy, making this a great spot to grab a quick bite to eat. A special includes a hamburger, fries, and soda for 1,590ISK, which is pretty cheap for a meal in downtown Reykjavík.

Hlölla Bátar (Ingólfstorg. 354/511-3500, www.hlollabatar.is, 11:30am-10pm daily, sandwiches from 890ISK) has hot and cold hero/hoagie sandwiches on offer, including barbecue, curry, ham and cheese, and veggie boats. It's a great place to get something quick to eat, fuel up, and continue exploring the city.

Islenska Hamborgarafabrikkan (Icelandic Hamburger Factory) (Höfðatún 2, tel. 354/575-7575, www.fabrikkan.is, 11am-10pm Sun.-Thurs., 11am-midnight Fri.-Sat., burgers from 1,695ISK) is a wildly popular hamburger joint. It has the look and feel of a casual eatery, but the hamburgers are pretty special. They range from classic hamburgers with lettuce, cheese, and tomatoes to more creative concoctions like the surf-and-turf, which combines a beef patty with tiger prawns, garlic, Japanese seaweed, cheese, lettuce, tomatoes, red onions, and garlic-cheese sauce. Other options include chicken and lamb, as well as a whale meat burger.

Roadhouse (Snorrabraut 56, tel. 354/571-4200, www.roadhouse.is, 11:30am-9:30pm Mon.-Thurs., 11:30am-11pm Fri.-Sat., noon-9:30pm Sun., burgers from 1,895ISK) does its best to depict an American-style hamburger joint. It's kitschy, cute, and familiar, with Americana hanging on the walls, ranging from old license plates to Elvis Presley posters. The food is exceptional "fast food," with choice burgers featuring everything from crumbled blue cheese to jalapeños and fried onions. A favorite among Icelanders is the Texas mac-and-cheese burger, with a patty, macaroni and cheese, bacon, and barbecue sauce piled on top. The pork baby-back ribs are memorable.

COFFEEHOUSES

Café Babalu (Skólavörðustígur 22, tel. 354/555-8845, www.babalu.is, 11am-11pm daily, 500ISK) is a charming coffeehouse decorated with vintage furniture, lots of wood furnishings, and kitschy knickknack goodness. Other than coffee drinks, the two-floor café serves light meals including soup, panini, and crepes. This is a favorite among tourists, and in the summer months, there's an outdoor eating area on the second floor.

Café Haiti (Geirsgata 7, tel. 354/588-8484, www.cafehaiti.is, 8am-8pm Mon.-Thurs., 8am-11pm Fri., 9am-11pm Sat., 9am-8pm Sun., light meals from 950ISK) is owned and operated by a delightful Haitian woman who has called Iceland home for years. The atmosphere is warm and inviting, with comfortable couches and chairs among the tables and even a little stage area upfront for regular concerts that take place. In addition to coffee and tea, light meals of soup and sandwiches are available, as well as sweet treats like cakes and cookies. A house favorite is specially brewed Arabic coffee that takes some time, but it's well worth the wait.

C Is for Cookie (Tysgata 8, tel. 354/578-5914, 9am-6pm Mon.-Fri., 11am-5pm Sat., noon-5pm Sun., 500ISK) is a nondescript café on a quiet side street in the city. For that reason, along with a stellar cup of coffee, it's a favorite among locals. When the weather is good, people congregate in a park adjacent to the coffeehouse and at tables and chairs outside. Freshly baked treats include Icelandic pancakes, brownies, and, of course, cookies.

Kaffitár (Bankastræti 8, tel. 354/511-4540, www.kaffitar.is, 7:30am-6pm Mon.-Sat., 9am-5pm Sun., 500ISK) is the closest thing Iceland has to a coffee chain like Dunkin Donuts or Starbucks. There are locations in city center, Keflavík airport, and a smattering of other sites. They also sell coffee beans and ground coffee in supermarkets and takeout coffee at gas stations. The city center location is bright, colorful, and usually crowded. The coffee is fresh and the cakes and other sweets are delicious. You can't go wrong at Kaffitár.

Mokka (Skólavörðustígur 3A, tel. 354/552-1174, www.mokka.is, 9am-6:30pm daily, 500ISK) is the oldest coffeehouse in Reykjavík and still has a faithful following today. It's busy all day, with tourists as well as artists, writers, and other famous folks stopping by for a cup of coffee and Mokka's famous waffles with fresh cream and homemade jam. Art and photography exhibitions are frequently held at the coffeehouse, so stop by and have a look at the walls.

Reykjavík Roasters (Karastigur 1, tel. 354/517-5535, www.reykjavikroasters.is, 8am-6pm Mon.-Fri., 9am-6pm Sat.-Sun., 500ISK) is a

Café Babalu

Mokka

charming corner coffeehouse situated in a great part of town. Just a stone's throw from Hallgrímskirkja, Reykjavík Roasters is a great spot to sit down for a coffee to break up a busy day of sightseeing. Decorated with vintage couches and chairs and wood tables with delicate tablecloths, the coffeehouse is packed with tourists and locals chilling out, drinking lattes and getting some good free Wi-Fi. During the summer months, when the weather is cooperating, there's an outside sitting area to all guests to enjoy their drinks while soaking in the sun.

Stofan Café (Vesturgata 3, tel. 354/863-8583, 101stofan@gmail.com, 9am-midnight Mon.-Thurs., 9am-1am Fri.-Sat., 10am-11pm Sun., 500ISK) moved to a larger space in 2014, closer to the harbor, and with more space came more couches, chairs, and tables to accommodate the growing number of fans of this hot spot. The café serves coffee drinks, local beers, and cakes and light meals. It's common to catch locals enjoying their drinks while curling up with a good book on a vintage armchair.

VEGETARIAN

Gló (Engjateigi 19, tel. 354/553-1111, www.glo.is, 11am-9pm daily, 2,500ISK) has a spectacular menu featuring not just vegetarian and vegan options, but also a killer raw food selection. Expect to see staples like tofu and hummus served in creative ways, and there's also a great salad bar. The meat dish option can be great if you're traveling with a carnivore. The decor is modern and chic and the staff friendly.

ICE CREAM

Eldur og Is (Skólavörðustígur 2, tel. 354/571-2480, 1,000ISK) offers soft-serve and Italian-style ice cream with flavors including the basics: vanilla, chocolate, and strawberry, as well as coffee, pistachio, and several others. A crepe bar inside has delicious combinations, including the Nutella and nut special crepe. This place has a central location and a good reputation, so it can be a bit crowded. The sofas and armchairs inside make it very comfortable.

Valdis (Grandagarður 21, tel. 354/586-8088, www.valdis.is, noon-11pm daily, from 330ISK) draws a crowd during sun-soaked summer days and the dim, windy dog days of winter. It's always busy here and for good reason. The harbor location and its creative and delicious ice cream flavors make this a favorite among locals and tourists. Flavors include coconut, white chocolate, vanilla coffee, Oreo, and local favorites black licorice and rhubarb. During the summer, there are tables and chairs outside the shop, where scores of people enjoy their cones.

Information and Services

VISITORS CENTERS

Around Iceland (Laugavegur 18b, tel. 354/561-9161, www.aroundiceland. is, 8am-7pm daily) is a lively tourist office with the regions of Iceland separated in different exhibitions. The sections are Reykjavík, West, South, East, and North Iceland, and brochures are available to help you explore each region. The friendly staff is eager to help you book afternoon, day, or multiday tours ranging from a Golden Circle tour (including visits to Gullfoss, Geysir, and Þingvellir) to hiking tours in North Iceland. There's something for everyone. In the front is an eclectic array of souvenirs, including jewelry and woolen goods, and in the back is a cozy coffeehouse with armchairs, sofas, coffee drinks, and light meals.

The Reykjavík tourist information center (Aðalstræti 2, tel. 354/590-1550, www.visitreykjavik.is, 8:30am-7pm daily June-mid-Sept., 9am-6pm Mon.-Fri., 9am-4pm Sat.-Sun. mid-Sept.-May) is a one-stop shop for all your tourist needs. The building is thought of as a hub, with brochures available for every region of the island and information on every tour on offer. You can pick up maps and purchase tickets to events.

MEDIA

The Reykjavík Grapevine is Iceland's only English-language newspaper, and it's geared toward tourists, hipsters, and music-loving locals. There are listings for bands and DJ club dates, information about what's on at museums and art galleries, and articles ranging from humorous to informative to sarcastic on what's going on in Reykjavík. To get the pulse of the city, pick up a copy in bookstores, museums, and shops, or check it out online at www.grapevine.is. In summertime, the newspaper comes out every other week, and in the winter it's monthly.

EMERGENCY SERVICES

The telephone number for emergencies is 112. If you are having a medical emergency, are stranded by car trouble, or are experiencing a safety issue or any other pressing, dire emergency, dial this number.

MEDICAL SERVICES

Landspitali (Norðurmýri, tel. 354/543-1000, www.landspitali.is) is the national hospital of Iceland. It houses day-patient units, an emergency room, and clinical services. If you are experiencing a medical emergency, dial 112 for an ambulance.

For a pharmacy, visit Lyf og Heilsa (Haaleitisbraut 68, tel. 354/581-2101, 8am-midnight Mon.-Fri., 10am-midnight Sat.-Sun.). Keep in mind that "over the counter" medication and aspirin are only available at a pharmacy, not in supermarkets or convenience stores like in other countries.

Transportation

GETTING THERE
Air

Iceland isn't as difficult to reach as you may think. Smack dab in the mid-Atlantic, Reykjavík is just a short flight for many North Americans and Europeans, about five hours from New York City and three hours from London. The majority of international travel is handled through Keflavík International Airport (KEF), which is about 50 minutes west of Reykjavík.

Reykjavík City Airport (Þorragata 10, tel. 354/569-4100, www.isavia.is) is the city's domestic airport, with regional connections to towns throughout the country, including Akureyri and the Westfjords. The only international flights are to the Faroe Islands and Greenland.

Several airlines have offices in Reykjavík: Air Iceland (Reykjavíkurflugvöllur, tel. 354/570-3000, www.airiceland.is), Eagle Air (Reykjavíkurflugvöllur, tel. 354/562-4200, www.eagleair.is), Icelandair (Reykjavíkurflugvöllur, tel. 354/505-0100, www.icelandair.is), and Wow Air (Katrinartun 12, tel. 354/590-3000, www.wowair.is).

GETTING TO AND FROM THE AIRPORT

The Fly Bus (tel. 354/580-5400, www.flybus.is) runs regularly from Keflavík International Airport to BSÍ (Vatnsmýrarvegur 10, tel. 354/562-1011, www.bsi.is), Reykjavík's main bus station, where you can get a shuttle to your hotel in Reykjavík. It takes about 50 minutes to get from Keflavík to BSÍ bus station, and buses depart about 40 minutes after flights land. One-way tickets cost 1,950ISK. (BSÍ is also the main departure site for day-tour bus trips with various companies, including Reykjavík Excursions.) Taxis are also available at Keflavík; the fare from the airport to Reykjavík is upward of 12,000ISK.

Strætó (www.straeto) bus numbers 15 and 19 stop at the Reykjavík City **55**
Airport near the Air Iceland and Eagle Air terminals, respectively. Taxis
are also available on-site.

GETTING AROUND
Bus

Reykjavík's bus system is convenient, reliable, and an affordable way to
get around the city. The bus system, called Strætó (www.straeto.is), which
means "street" in Icelandic, runs about 30 bus lines within the city center
as well as to outlying Reykjavík areas like Kópavogur and Hafnarfjörður.
The bright yellow buses cost 400ISK per ride within the city limits, and
you can ask for a free bus transfer if you need to switch buses to get to
your destination. You must pay with exact change; bus drivers don't make
change. Buses run daily 7am-11pm. Be sure to check the website at www.
straeto.is for information on holiday schedules and delays due to weather.

If you plan to use the bus a fair amount, you can buy nine tickets
for 3,500ISK at Hlemmur bus station (Laugavegur, tel. 354/540-2701).
Hlemmur is Strætó's central downtown station, where you can catch or
connect to any bus you're looking for. Think of it as Reykjavík's equivalent
of New York's Times Square subway station. Another great option is the
Reykjavík Welcome Card, which grants you free access to the city's swimming pools, almost all the city's museums, and unlimited city bus rides.
You can purchase a card for one or three days for 1,000ISK and 2,500ISK,
respectively. If you will be spending a lot of time in Reykjavík, this is a
great option to save a lot of money. Cards can be purchased at tourist offices and bus stations.

Strætó's blue long-distance buses depart from Mjodd station (tel.
354/557-7854), eight kilometers southeast of city center, traveling to several regions around the country.

Taxi

The two things you need to know about taxis in Reykjavík is that they are
expensive and you have to call ahead for one. Hreyfill (tel. 354/588-5522,
www.hreyfill.is) and BSR (tel. 354/561-0000, www.taxireykjavik.is) are two
popular taxi companies in the city. Taxis arrive 5-10 minutes after you call,
and the price on the meter is inclusive—you don't tip in Iceland. It's rare to
spend less than 2,000ISK on a taxi ride, even for short distances. Cab prices
rival those in New York City. There are a couple of cab stations downtown
where you don't have to call ahead—just outside Hlemmur bus station and
near Lækjartorg. They are hard to miss as the line of taxis can be 10 deep.

Car

There is no shortage of rental car companies in Iceland eager to rent
you a car, and many of them make it quite easy, with offices at Keflavík
International Airport, BSÍ bus station, and around the city. They include
the following: Avis (Knarrarvogur 2, tel. 354/591-4000, www.avis.is),

TRANSPORTATION

Budget (Vatsmýrarvegur 10, tel. 354/562-6060, www.budget.is), Europcar (Hjallahrauni 9, tel. 354/565-3800, www.europcar.is), and Hertz (Reykjavík City Airport, tel. 354/505-0600, www.hertz.is).

Be advised that parking isn't easy in Reykjavík. Most locals have cars, and street parking can take some time. However, there are several parking garages and lots available around the city, and parking at a garage will cost less than 100ISK per hour.

Bicycle

Reykjavík has taken great strides in becoming more bicycle-friendly over the past few years. There are new bicycle lanes throughout the city as well as new bike racks to lock up your ride outside shops. Be aware that bike theft is rampant, so be proactive and lock up your bicycle. Don't leave it unattended and unlocked. It'll disappear. Other than bike theft, the only other concern for cyclists is weather, which changes often. You can start your ride during calm and sunny skies, but within minutes that could change with rain and wind.

One of the most central and most popular bike rental companies in Reykjavík is Borgarhjol Bike Rental (Hverfisgata 50, tel. 354/551-5653, www.borgarhjol.is), close to the main street Laugavegur. Bike rentals begin at 2,600ISK for four hours.

Walking

Reykjavík is an inherently walkable city, depending on the weather, of course. Because of its small size, it's a perfect city to roam, to pop into quaint shops, visit museums, and photograph the many statues around the city. You can start at the harbor and make your way to Tjörnin, up to Hallgrímskirkja, and beyond.

A new walking tour was launched in 2013 by I Heart Reykjavík (Mjóahlíð 14, tel. 354/854-4476, www.iheartreykjavik.net) that is designed to tell you about the history of Reykjavík and some of the quirky characters who inhabit the city. It's a three-hour tour for 5,000ISK, and you can book at www.tours.iheartreykjavik.net. Tours are offered daily.

MOSFELLSBÆR

Just 15 minutes from downtown Reykjavík, Mosfellsbær is a quaint, placid town with a picturesque bay, beautiful mountains, and clean streams and rivers. About 9,000 people live in Mosfellsbær, and it feels remote enough to feel like you're closer to the countryside, but it's also close enough to get downtown.

Sights
ÁLAFOSS WOOL FACTORY SHOP

The **Álafoss Wool Factory Shop** (Álafossvegur 23, tel. 354/566-6303, www. alafoss.is, 9am-6pm Mon.-Fri., 9am-4pm Sat.) is home to the Álafoss wool brand, which was established in 1896. The shop sells wool skeins, scarves, hats, sweaters, and blankets, along with some other small goods. You can also purchase a sheep skin as well as other Icelandic design products. The shop is located in the old factory house by the Álafoss waterfall, which was used to drive the mills of the old factory. For decades it was the leading manufacturer and exporter of Icelandic wool products. You can visit to experience this important side of Iceland's industrial history and get a look at an exhibition of old knitting machinery and photographs from the early days. The prices are comparable to downtown Reykjavík prices, but the selection is better and bigger.

GLJÚFRASTEINN

Gljúfrasteinn (Pósthólf 250, tel. 354/568-8066, www.gljufrasteinn.is, 9am-5pm daily June-Aug., 10am-5pm Tues.-Sun. Sept.-May, 800ISK) was the home of Icelandic novelist and national treasure Halldór Laxness. Laxness, who was awarded the Nobel Prize for Literature in 1955 for his novel *Independent People,* lived at this home from 1945 until his death in 1998. It has been preserved as a museum, giving visitors a glimpse into his life, including his library and study, where he wrote several of his works. There is a short multimedia presentation about his life and work, available in English, Icelandic, and Swedish. Guided tours of the house and grounds take about an hour. You can purchase many of his books at the museum, translated into English and German. The house, which is a white two-story concrete building, is well preserved, but it feels lived in with lots of personal artifacts decorating the home, including books, clothing, and furniture.

Sports and Recreation
★ HIKING MOUNT ESJA

Standing 914 meters high, Mount Esja looms over Reykjavík, and it's a favorite among locals and the subject of thousands of picturesque photographs snapped by tourists. Hiking Esja is a popular pastime and a few paths ascend the mountain. The most popular path begins at the car park,

Greater Reykjavík

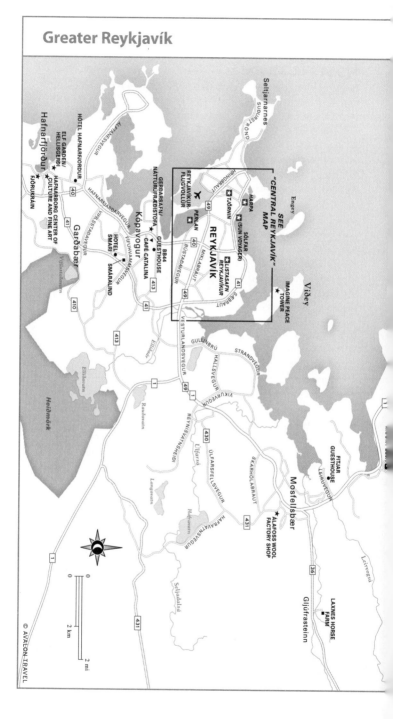

Seltjarnarnes

Engey

Viðey

"SEE
"CENTRAL
REYKJAVÍK"
MAP"

REYKJAVÍK
FLUGVÖLLUR

HARPA

TJÖRNIN

SÓLFAR
(SUN VOYAGER)

PERLAN

LISTASAFN
REYKJAVÍKUR

IMAGINE PEACE
TOWER

HOTEL HAFNARFJÖRÐUR

ELF GARDEN/
HELLISGERÐI

HAFNARBORG CENTER OF
CULTURE AND FINE ART

FJÖRUKRÁIN

Hafnarfjörður

Garðabær

GERÐARSAFN/
NÁTTÚRUFRÆÐISTOFA

BB44
GUESTHOUSE

CAFÉ CATALINA

HOTEL
SMÁRI

SMÁRALIND

Kópavogur

Heiðmörk

Elliðaár

Elliðavatn

Rauðavatn

Langavatn

Hafravatn

Seljadalur

GULLINBRÚ

HALLSVEGUR

STRANDVEGUR

VESTURLANDSVEGUR

VÍKURVEGUR

REYNISVATNSHEIÐI

ÚLFARSFELLSVEGUR

HAFRAVATNSVEGUR

Úlfarsá

SKARHÓLABRAUT

ÁLAFOSS WOOL
FACTORY SHOP

Mosfellsbær

FITJAR
GUESTHOUSE

LEIRVOGUR

Leirvogsá

Gljúfrasteinn

LAXNES HORSE
FARM

HÁFNARFJARÐARVEGUR

ÁLFTANESVEGUR

HRINGBRAUT

MIKLABRAUT

BÚSTAÐAVEGUR

SÆBRAUT

0
0
2 km
2 mi

© AVALON TRAVEL

which is at about 780 meters. From there, you can cross the Mógilsa stream, which leads to a steeper stretch named "steinnin." The hike is eight kilometers round-trip and it's considered easy, but be aware that the last stretch to the top is pretty steep. There are handrails to lessen the challenge. When you reach the top of this path, there is a guestbook to sign. It's fun to read through all the names and see where people have traveled from to climb the mountain.

Please be careful before you head out. Make sure you check the weather forecast and let your guesthouse or hotel know of your plans. Remember that the weather can be fickle. It can be beautiful out with sunny skies, but it could turn very windy and rainy. Make sure you bring water, proper footwear, and waterproof clothing with you.

Getting to Esja is pretty easy, even if you don't have access to a car. It's just 20 minutes (10.7 kilometers) north of Mosfellsbær and is accessible from Route 1. Drive through Mosfellsbær and you will see the signs pointing to the car park. By bus, you can take the **Strætó** 57 bus (www.straeto. is) from the bus station Mjodd in Reykjavík. The bus fare is 800ISK and the bus departs 12 times a day. It's a 30-minute ride. Let the bus driver know that you are heading to the base of Esja (the bus stop is Esjumelar) and you will get dropped off at the car park.

HORSE RIDING

If you're staying in Reykjavík and want to do some local horse riding, **Laxnes Farm** (off Rte. 36, tel. 354/566-6179, www.laxnes.is) is just a 15-minute drive northeast from downtown Reykjavík. Icelandic horses are available to ride for different tour lengths. The staff is warm and friendly and shows a great deal of love and respect for the horses they care for. A popular tour is called the "Laxnes Special"; you will be picked up at your hotel or guesthouse in Reykjavík and taken to the farm, where you will meet your guide and horse. You are given all the gear you need, including helmets, rain clothes, and boots, and are taken on a glorious two-hour riding tour (9,900ISK) that has spectacular landscape views. The Laxnes Farm is close to Halldór Laxness's home, but they are not related.

SWIMMING

If you're planning to stay in town for a few hours or more, check out the local swimming pool, called **Varmárlaug** (Þverholt 2, tel. 354/566-6754, 6:30am-8pm Mon.-Fri., 9am-6pm Sat.-Sun. in summer, 4pm-9pm Mon.-Fri. in winter, 600ISK). The pool isn't as impressive as some of the pools in Reykjavík city center, but the water is warm and the facilities are clean. You're likely to see locals taking a dip, but not many tourists.

Accommodations

Fitjar Guesthouse (Fitjar, tel. 354/691-5005, www.fitjarguesthouse. com, rooms from 9,000ISK) is a six-room guesthouse on a quiet street in Mosfellsbær. Three rooms have private bathroom facilities with a shower, and three rooms share bathroom accommodations. Rooms are clean and comfortable, but the decor is nothing to write home about. This is a great spot to spend a night before you continue on your journey. Guests have access to free Wi-Fi, a television, a common, fully equipped kitchen, and laundry facilities.

Food

Kaffihúsið Álafossi (Álafossvegur 27, tel. 354/566-8030, www.alaborg.is, 11am-10pm Mon.-Fri., 11am-7pm Sat., noon-7pm Sun., 1,500ISK) is a cozy coffeehouse right next to the Álafoss Wool Factory Shop. It serves light meals ranging from soups to sandwiches. The staff is warm and there's interesting artwork from local Icelandic artists adorning the walls. The coffee and cakes are splendid.

Mosfellsbakarí (Háholt 13-15, tel. 354/566-6145, www.mosbak.is, 7am-6pm Mon.-Fri., 8am-4pm Sat.-Sun., pastries from 600ISK) is a decadent bakery known for its chocolate creations. Located in the center of town, the bakery does roaring business. In addition to its indulgent cakes and pastries, the bakery offers light meals, including sandwiches and soup.

Information and Services

Mosfellsbær's **tourist information office** is based inside the **Mosfellsbær public library** (Þverholt 2, tel. 354/566-6822, www.mosfellsbaer.is, 9am-5pm daily), which is housed inside a shopping area. It's a great place to stop to gather some tourist brochures and maps as well as buy some food at the grocery store inside the shopping center.

Getting There and Around

Mosfellsbær is just a 15-minute drive from downtown Reykjavík. It's 14 kilometers northeast of Reykjavík via Route 49.

By bus, take the 15 bus to the Haholt stop, which is in the center of town. Check www.straeto.is for more bus information. Depending on the time of day, buses run every 30 minutes to every hour, and it takes 30 minutes from downtown Reykjavík to Mosfellsbær. A single ride on the bus is 400ISK.

KÓPAVOGUR

Kópavogur is a quiet suburb home to families, young professionals, and immigrants, and it attracts people traveling on business or shoppers headed to the Smáralind mall or the island's only IKEA. There are a couple of museums worth checking out for local art and history.

Sights

GERÐARSAFN (KÓPAVOGUR ART MUSEUM)

The **Kópavogur Art Museum** (Hamraborg 4, tel. 354/570-0440, www. gerdarsafn.is, 11am-5pm Tues.-Sun., 500ISK) is named Gerðarsafn in Icelandic, after sculptor Gerður Helgadóttir, who passed away in 1975. In 1977, her heirs donated roughly 1,400 of her works to the municipality of Kópavogur on the condition that a museum bearing her name would be opened. Gerður's black-iron works in the 1950s made her a pioneer of three-dimensional abstract art in Iceland. Around 1970 Gerður returned to working with plaster, terra cotta, and concrete, using simple circles with movement in many variations. The museum opened in 1994. Other works on display range from contemporary to landscape art. It's a pretty museum with varied works of art, and it's worth a visit if you're in the neighborhood.

NÁTTÚRÚFRÆÐISTOFA (NATURAL HISTORY MUSEUM)

The **Natural History Museum** (Hamraborg 6A, tel. 354/570-0430, www. natkop.is, 10am-7pm Mon.-Thurs., 11am-5pm Fri., 1pm-5pm Sat., free) opened its doors in 2002 and is a great place to bring kids to learn about the animals and geology of Iceland. The museum exhibitions fall into two categories: zoological and geological. The geology section, where you learn about the major rock types and minerals of Iceland, is of more interest to adults. The zoological part focuses on the mammals, fish, birds, and invertebrates of Iceland. It's educational and entertaining, and kids love it due to the various exhibitions on seals, foxes, and cute birds like puffins.

Sports and Recreation
SWIMMING

The **Kópavogur Swimming Pool** (Borgarholtsbraut 17, tel. 354/540-0470, 6:30am-10pm Mon.-Fri., 8am-7pm Sat.-Sun., 500ISK) is frequented by locals and their children and has a very family-friendly atmosphere. Amenities include a 50-meter outdoor pool, two smaller indoor pools, three water slides, seven hot pots, and a steam bath. You aren't likely to see crowds or tourists, so if you're looking to just swim, this is a good spot.

Accommodations

Hótel Smári (Hlíðarsmára, tel. 354/558-1900, www.hotelsmari.is, rooms from 25,000ISK) is a 48-room block hotel situated right next to the huge mall Smáralind. The rooms are in need of an update, as they have an 1980s style with carpeting, orange hues, ad shiny lamps. But the rooms are clean and spacious, and comfortable for a short stay.

BB44 Guesthouse (Borgarholtsbraut 44/Nýbýlavegur 16, tel. 354/554 4228, www.bb44.is, doubles 11,300ISK) offers eight guest rooms in two locations. The single, double, and family rooms have free Wi-Fi, shared kitchen facilities, and free parking. Rooms are very basic, with standard beds, desks, and simple chairs. The location is prime, just a 10-minute walk from downtown Kópavogur, where there are museums, restaurants, and the town's swimming pool. Guests have access to a hot tub at the guesthouse.

Food

Café Catalina (Hamraborg 11, tel. 354/554-2166, www.catalina.is, 11am-9pm Mon.-Fri., noon-3am Sat.-Sun., 1,500ISK) offers Icelandic comfort food at decent prices. The menu includes mashed fish with rye bread, fishballs with potatoes and onion sauce, and Icelandic meat soup. Other options include hamburgers, sandwiches, and soups. There's live music on the weekends, which draws plenty of locals.

Smáralind (Hagasmara 1, tel. 354/528-8000, www.smaralind.is, 11am-7pm Mon., Wed., and Fri., 11am-9pm Thurs., 11am-6pm Sat., 1pm-6pm Sun.) is Iceland's largest shopping mall, and in addition to a food court, there are casual eateries TGI Friday's and Café Adesso, coffee shop Kaffitár, and Serrano, which serves Mexican-style food.

Information and Services

The town's service and administration center (Fannborg 2, tel. 354/570-1500) is open 8am-4pm Monday-Thursday and 8am-3pm Friday.

Getting There and Around

Kópavogur is just a 10-minute ride south from downtown Reykjavík by car. You take Route 40 to Route 49 and it's 5 kilometers.

City buses go to Kópavogur, including buses 1, 2, and 28. Buses leave every 30 minutes or so, the fare is 400ISK for one way, and it takes about 20 minutes by bus. Check www.straeto.is for more bus information.

HAFNARFJÖRÐUR

Hafnarfjörður is a picturesque fishing town that about 30,000 people call home. Attractions include a scenic harbor, pretty parks, and the famous Viking Village, a restaurant and hotel that plays host to numerous Viking-related events.

Sights

HAFNARFJÖRÐUR MUSEUM

Hafnarfjörður Museum (Vesturgata 8, www.hafnarfjordur.is, 11am-5pm daily June-Aug., 11am-5pm Sat.-Sun. rest of year, 600ISK) houses a

Hafnarfjörður

collection of cultural artifacts and photographs that are significant to the town. The museum consists of six houses and nine exhibitions that showcase how life was in the town in the old days. The six houses date from 1803 to 1906 and include the oldest house in the town, Sivertsen's House.

HAFNARBORG CENTER OF CULTURE AND FINE ART

Hafnarborg Center of Culture and Fine Art (Strandgata 34, tel. 354/555-0800, www.hafnarborg.is, noon-5pm Wed.-Mon., 500ISK) consists of two exhibition galleries with rotating exhibitions ranging from contemporary art from modern Icelandic artists to works by some of the island's most celebrated artists of years past.

FJÖRUKRÁIN (VIKING VILLAGE)

Fjörukráin (Viking Village) (Strandgata 55, tel. 354/565-1213, www.vikingvillage.is) is great fun for kids and adults alike. The closest thing Iceland has to a theme park, the Viking Village celebrates the island's history, with a sense of humor. It's kitschy, with lots of Viking horns, reproduced wood huts, and wooden furnishings. Guests can stay at the hotel, visit the gift shop, stay for a meal at the restaurant, or just check out the decor.

The Viking Village takes center stage every mid-June when the space hosts the **Viking Festival,** which takes place over five days. There are performances of jousts with participants in Viking costumes, food stands, metalwork demonstrations, and woolen goods and jewelry for sale.

Sports and Recreation

SWIMMING

Take a dip with the locals at the **Suðurbæjarlaug** pool (Hringbraut 77, tel. 354/565-3080, 6:30am-9:30pm Mon.-Fri., 8am-5:30pm Sat.-Sun., 500ISK), which has an outdoor pool with a water slide, a steam bath, and a few hot tubs.

HORSE RIDING

This town is a lovely place to ride a horse. With its rolling landscape and picturesque views, it doesn't get much better than this in the greater Reykjavík area. **Íshestar** (Sörlaskeið 26, tel. 354/555-7000, www.ishestar.is) is a local company that offers an array of tours. They provide transportation to the riding center from your accommodation and all gear needed to ride. A half-day tour goes for about 17,000ISK.

Accommodations

Hótel Hafnarfjörður (Reykjavíkurvegur 72, tel. 354/540-9700, www.hhotel.is, rooms from 16,000ISK) is a 70-room hotel with comfortable rooms ranging from single rooms to family suites. The hotel has a business traveler/corporate feel to it, but you can't beat the amenities and location. Rooms feature neutral hues, simple furnishings, and private bathrooms.

Some rooms have a kitchenette for self-catering needs. Continental breakfast, Wi-Fi, parking, and access to a nearby fitness center are included in the price.

Hótel Viking (Strandgata 55, tel. 354/565-1213, www.vikingvillage.is, rooms from 18,300ISK) at the Viking Village has 42 hotel rooms and 14 "Viking cottages" next to the hotel. All rooms and cottages include private bathrooms, comfortable beds, televisions, and stylish Viking accessories. The hotel features artworks from Iceland, Greenland, and the Faroe Islands, which is a lot of fun. Guests have access to free Wi-Fi, free parking, and a hot tub on-site. Breakfast is included in the price.

Food

Fjörugarðurinn (Viking Restaurant) (Strandagata 55, tel. 354/565-1213, www.fjorukrain.is, 2,400ISK) at the Viking Village is a restaurant that serves traditional Icelandic fare like lamb and fish dishes in a fun, Viking-themed atmosphere. There are lots of wood furnishings and medieval accents displayed throughout the space. You can book a Viking performance in advance for large groups for a fee, which includes the guests being "kidnapped" from their bus, brought into a "cave" in the restaurant, served mead, escorted to dinner, and entertained with singing and music. The restaurant is open for dinner 6pm-10pm daily.

Osushi (Reykjarvíkurvegur 60, tel. 354/561-0562, www.osushi.is, 11:30am-9:30pm Mon.-Thurs., 11:30am-10pm Fri.-Sat., 3pm-9:30pm Sun., bites from 300ISK) is the Hafnarfjörður outpost of the popular downtown Reykjavík sushi train. Individual bites on offer range from fresh salmon farmed from Iceland's shores to eel and shrimp-based pieces.

Súfistinn (Strandgata 9, tel. 354/565-3740, 8am-11:30pm Mon.-Thurs., 8am-midnight Fri., 10am-midnight Sat., 1pm-midnight Sun., 800ISK) is a cozy café that sells stellar coffee drinks, fresh pastries, and light meals. Situated by the central downtown shopping area and performance hall, it's a perfect place to grab a blueberry muffin and latte or a soup or sandwich.

Information and Services

The tourist information center is situated in **Hafnarfjörður Town Hall** (Strandgata 6, tel. 354/585-5555, www.hafnarfjordur.is, 8am-5pm Mon.-Fri. year-round, 10am-3pm Sat.-Sun. June-Aug.). You can arrange for transportation, buy tickets to local tours, and peruse brochures about the town's sights.

Getting There and Around

Hafnarfjörður is just a 15-minute drive south from downtown Reykjavík. It's an 11-kilometer drive, and you take Route 40 to get there.

City bus 1 stops in town. Check www.straeto.is for bus schedules and information.

Viðey is a little gem of an island accessible by ferry. Historically, the island was inhabited by an Augustine monastery from 1225 to 1539 and was the center for a pilgrimage in the Middle Ages. The island is home to one of the oldest buildings in Iceland—Viðeyjarstofa (Höfuðborgarsvæði), which dates back to 1755 and served as a home to many of Iceland's most powerful men over generations. The building is a white stone building with a black roof, and it's open to the public. The island, which is just 1.6 square kilometers in size, hosts unspoiled nature with vast stretches of grassy plains and rich birdlife, as well as the John Lennon Peace Tower, an installation created by Yoko Ono.

Imagine Peace Tower

The Imagine Peace Tower (www.imaginepeacetower.com) is an outdoor installation created by artist Yoko Ono in memory of her late husband, John Lennon. A light beams from a structure into the sky, visible from miles away. It was unveiled on Viðey on October 9, 2007, which was Lennon's 67th birthday. It's lit every year from October 9, Lennon's birthday, until December 8, the anniversary of Lennon's death. The words "imagine peace" are inscribed on the structure in 24 languages. The base of the tower is 10 meters wide, and the beam of light reaches 4,000 meters into the sky.

Getting There and Around

In the summer, Elding (tel. 354/533-5055, www.videy.com) operates a ferry with eight daily departures mid-May through September from Skarfabakki pier, Harpa, and Ægisgarður pier. Ferries run in the afternoon. During the rest of the year the ferry runs three departures on Saturdays and Sundays from Skarfabakki to Viðey. The ferry ride costs 1,100ISK and is just about 10 minutes.

Viðey Island

Reykjanes Peninsula

The Reykjanes Peninsula is home to a striking, dramatic landscape that has lava fields for miles, volcanic craters, geothermal waters and hot springs, and lava caves. The region is also a hotbed for outdoor activities, including horse riding, hiking, and bathing in hot springs.

REYKJANESBÆR (KEFLAVÍK AND NJARÐVÍK)

Reykjanesbær is where every tourist's journey begins in Iceland, as it is home to the country's only international airport, Keflavík.

During World War II, British and American troops arrived in Iceland and built the country's first airport base. Situated in between the United States and continental Europe, Iceland's location served the Allies well. Some may be surprised to learn that the last American troops left the island only in 2006.

While it may be tempting to get off the plane and get on a bus straight to Reykjavík, Reykjanesbær, which is a municipality that includes the towns Keflavík and Njarðvík, is a great place to explore. Lava fields for miles, coupled with majestic sea cliffs and accessible hiking trails, make the region a perfect place to roam. Throw on some hiking boots and have your camera ready. It's also a great spot for bird-watching during the summer months, when you can see arctic terns and gannets.

Sights

REYKJANES FOLK MUSEUM

Reykjanes Folk Museum (Duusgata 2-8, Keflavík, tel. 354/421-6700, www.reykjanes.is, 11am-6pm daily, 500ISK) hosts a variety of exhibits highlighting the town's rich history as one of Iceland's main commercial ports, and it remains so today. A museum housed in a stone turf-roofed farm cottage shows how life was lived in the region at the turn of the 20th century. On display are reconstructed rooms with vintage furnishings and artifacts, including furniture, cooking equipment, and work gear for fishermen.

REYKJANES ART MUSEUM

The Reykjanes Art Museum (Duusgata 2-8, Keflavík, tel. 354/421-6700, www.listasafn.reykjanesbaer.is, noon-5pm Mon.-Fri., 1pm-5pm Sat.-Sun., free) is a charming museum that hosts exhibitions of local artists and crafters. The museum gives a taste of the local and eclectic art scene. Check out contemporary art as well as traditional paintings of the rolling landscape.

REYKJANES MARITIME CENTER

The Reykjanes Maritime Center (Duusgata 2, Keflavík, tel. 354/421-6700, noon-5pm Mon.-Fri., 1pm-5pm Sat.-Sun., free), which opened in 2002, houses 100 model boats built by a retired local sailor, Grímur Karlsson. Models on display include masted schooners of the mid-19th century and

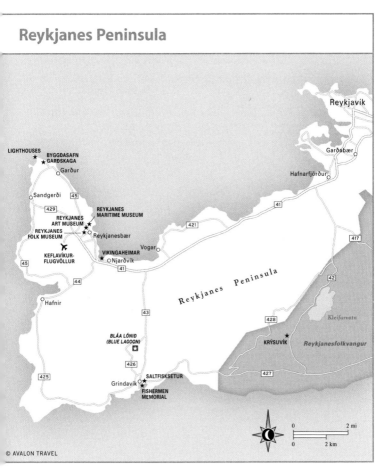

© AVALON TRAVEL

steam-powered trawlers of the 20th century. Information is available on the types of boats and when they were used.

VIKINGAHEIMAR (VIKING WORLD)

The museum **Viking World** (Vikingabraut 1, Njarðvík, tel. 354/894-2874, www.vikingaheimar.com, 1pm-4pm Mon.-Wed. and Sat.-Sun., 1,200ISK) is centered around a Viking ship exhibit. The ship *Íslendingur (Icelander)* was built in 2000 to sail to Greenland from Iceland to commemorate Leifur Eiríksson's trip to North America, and information is provided on the trip. It's a great photo op of a large replica of a Viking ship. The ship is housed inside a grand building with huge windows not too far from shore. Lifted several feet from the ground, the ship can be viewed from many interesting angles. A video exhibit shows how Viking ships were constructed. There are tables and chairs below, and you can spend some time gazing at the boat with the ocean in the background. When the weather is pleasant, it's great to sit on the large grass field and enjoy a coffee from the café inside. For kids, there's a "settlement zoo" exhibit, which allows children to get up close and personal with baby lambs, calves, and birds.

Sports and Recreation
WHALE-WATCHING
During the summer months (June-September), **Airport Whale Watching** (tel. 354/421-7777, www.dolphin.is, 8,000ISK for 3-hour trip) runs a tour from Keflavík Harbor. You have a chance to see dolphins and minke, fin, orca, sei, and humpback whales. The tours are three hours long on a large, 90-person vessel. If you do not see any whales or dolphins, you will be given a free voucher for another tour.

SWIMMING
The **Vatnaveröld Swimming Pool** (Sunnubraut 31, Keflavík, tel. 354/421-1500, 7am-8pm Mon.-Fri., 8am-6pm Sat.-Sun., 400ISK) in Keflavík is complete with hot tubs, heated pools, and a great swimming area for children. It's a wildly popular spot for locals and gives you a peek into an integral part of Icelandic society.

Events
The major touring music festival **All Tomorrow's Parties** (www.atpfestival.com) found its way to Iceland a few years ago. Local and international acts take the stage at Ásbrú (former NATO base) in Keflavík for three days in early July. Past performers include Nick Cave, Neil Young, and Interpol.

Accommodations
One of the busiest hostels outside of Reykjavík, **FIT Hostel** (Fitjabraut 6A, Keflavík, tel. 354/421-8889, www.fithostel.is, beds from 4,000ISK) is where many begin their journey. Located just a few minutes from the airport, the 100-bed hostel offers rooms that sleep 2-6 people, common kitchen areas, shared bathrooms, and laundry facilities. It's not pretty by any means, but beds are cheap and it's a great place to meet fellow travelers who are looking to share rides and gas costs. Private double rooms cost 7,900ISK, and dorm accommodation is 4,000ISK.

At **Hótel Berg** (Bakkavegur 17, Keflavík, tel. 354/422-7922, www.hotelberg.is, rooms from 11,000ISK), the 17 rooms are comfortable and have flat-screen televisions and free Wi-Fi. The decor is a bit old-fashioned, with tasseled lampshades and grandmother quilts, but the queen-size beds are comfortable and the rooms clean. If you get one of the two loft suites during the winter months, you might catch a glimpse of the northern lights from the skylight.

The 68 rooms at **Hótel Keflavík** (Vatnsvegur 12, Keflavík, tel. 354/420-7000, www.hotelkeflavik.is, rooms from 34,000ISK) are a bit small, but each has a private bathroom, comfortable beds, and great views of the landscape. Guests are treated to a warm and helpful staff. An in-house restaurant serves traditional Icelandic fare and some international favorites.

Keflavík's 20-room, centrally located modern hotel, Hótel Keilir (Hafnargata 37, Keflavík, tel. 354/420-9800, www.eng.hotelkelir.is, rooms from 14,900ISK), boasts minimalist decor, average-sized rooms, and small bathrooms. A family suite is available that comfortably sleeps five people.

Icelandair Hótel-Keflavík (Hafnargata 57, Keflavík, tel. 354/421-5222, www.icelandairhotels.com, rooms from 32,000ISK) is just 10 minutes from the airport and a 15-minute drive to the Blue Lagoon. The 60-room hotel offers modern and comfortable rooms, an in-house spa, and a restaurant.

Food
Situated in the heart of the town, Langbest (Hafnargata 62, Keflavík, tel. 354/421-4777, www.langbest.is, 11:30am-9:30pm daily, 1,000ISK) serves up pizza, sandwiches, and fish-and-chips. It's a great place to stop for something quick and affordable.

Housed in Icelandair Hótel's Keflavík location, Vocal Restaurant (Hafnargata 57, Keflavík, tel. 354/421-5222, www.icehotels.is, 5am-10pm daily, 1,900ISK) is known for serving classic fish and meat dishes. Expect to see classic Icelandic cod, salmon, and lamb recipes on the menu. It opens for breakfast at 5am for early birds.

Information and Services
Reykjanesbær's tourist office (Hafnargata 57, tel. 354/421-6777, www.reykjanes.is, 10am-10pm daily June-Aug., 10am-4pm daily Sept.-May) is based in an office in the Reykjanesbær library.

Getting There and Around
Reykjanesbær is 49 kilometers southwest from Reykjavík. By car, take Route 41 to reach the region. It's about a 45-minute drive.

The Fly Bus (tel. 354/580-5400, www.flybus.is) runs regularly from Keflavík International Airport to the BSÍ bus station in Reykjavík, where you can get a shuttle to your hotel in Reykjavík. It takes about 50 minutes to get from Keflavík to BSÍ bus station, and buses depart about 40 minutes after flights land. One-way tickets cost 1,950ISK.

If you are staying in Reykjanesbær, be sure to contact your hotel or guesthouse to see if there is a shuttle to pick you up at the airport. If not, taxis are available at the airport.

There are tours for sights in Reykjanesbær, but if you want the freedom to roam, renting a car is essential.

GARÐUR
Garður is a placid seaside town on the northwest tip of Reykjanes and a great place to spend a couple of hours. Garður is best known for a pair

of lighthouses. On sunny summer days, you can see locals and tourists picnicking by the lighthouses, basking in the sun and enjoying the serenity and scenery. The lighthouses are a great spot to catch a glimpse of the northern lights in the winter, as the location is away from the bright lights of downtown.

Sights
LIGHTHOUSES

The main highlight of Garður is the two lighthouses, each with unique charm. The older, more traditional red-striped lighthouse was built in 1847, and the newer square-designed one was built in 1944 in a more modern Nordic design. This is a popular destination to stop and take a photo. Fishing boats can often be seen from shore, and there is rich birdlife in the region, ranging from hordes of seagulls circling in the summer months to ravens dominating the skies in the winter. It's also common to see arctic terns and gannets in the summer months. In the winter, the lighthouses appear against a backdrop of mist and mystery, and if you're lucky, you will see northern lights dancing in the night sky.

BYGGÐASAFN GARÐSKAGA (FOLK MUSEUM)

The **Byggðasafn Garðskaga (Folk Museum)** (Skagabraut 100, tel. 354/422-7220, www.svgardur.is, 1pm-5pm daily Apr.-Oct., open by appointment the rest of the year, free) is based in the rugged landscape with thriving birdlife. The quaint museum houses items that were essential for the livelihood of residents on both land and sea, including tools, fishing items, and maps. It offers a window into what life was like in past generations, reminding visitors that life in Iceland was not easy for early settlers. The museum also has an extensive collection of 60 functional engines provided by local resident Guðni Ingimundarson.

Sports and Recreation
CAMPING

There is a **free campground** (Skagabraut, tel. 354/422-7220) situated close to the two lighthouses. Campers have access to running water and toilets.

Accommodations and Food

Guesthouse Garður (Skagabraut 46, tel. 354/660-7894, www.guesthouse-gardur.is, apartments from 26,000ISK) is a charming guesthouse with seven apartments ranging from studios to two-bedrooms available year-round. Close to the harbor, the apartments have private kitchens, bathrooms with showers, free Wi-Fi, and satellite TV. The friendly staff can help arrange for local tours, including golfing, bird-watching, and fishing. The cozy guesthouse is just a 10-minute drive to Keflavík airport.

Getting There and Around

Garður is 55 kilometers west of Reykjavík. By car, take Route 41 to Route 45.

ELDEY ISLAND

Situated about 15 kilometers southwest from the southernmost tip of the Reykjanes Peninsula, Eldey Island is made up of sheer cliffs that jut out of the ocean and reach 77 meters high. Birdlife thrives on the island; Eldey has one of the biggest gannet bird colonies in the world. In recent years, an estimated 70,000 gannets have bred on the island from June to August. The best view of the island is from the Reykjanes Lighthouse; the GPS coordinates are N 63.8151, W 22.7033.

GRINDAVÍK

Grindavík is a placid fishing town steeped in fish trade history. Many of the same families have been trolling these waters for generations, and visitors can see fishers hauling their daily bounty of cod out of the harbor by day and dine on the local catch at night. The Grindavík area's greatest claim to fame, however, is the giant manmade geothermal expanse of the Blue Lagoon.

Sights

★ BLÁA LÓNIÐ (BLUE LAGOON)

Located 23 kilometers south of Keflavík International Airport, the **Blue Lagoon** (Svartsengi, tel. 354/420-8800, www.bluelagoon.com, 7:30am-9pm daily June-Aug., 10am-8pm daily Sept.-May) draws visitors from around the world, to soak in the glorious, healing waters amid a dreamlike atmosphere.

A trip to the Blue Lagoon in the winter is eerie and wonderful. Watching as snow falls from the jet-black December sky, or as northern lights dance across it, while soaking in the heated water is sublime. But the heated water, which ranges 37-39°C (98-102°F), is heavenly during any time of year. The milky waters and the misty air during the summer are lovely, especially on sunny days.

the Blue Lagoon

The water is not deep, less than five feet, and the bottom is covered with white silica mud, the result of a natural process of re-condensation. It's common to see visitors cover their faces with the mud, as it's very good for your skin. The gift shop sells Blue Lagoon skin products that have ingredients ranging from silica mud to algae found in other parts of Iceland.

For those not interested in taking a soak, there are two steam baths on the property, as well as a dry sauna and massage area. Spa treatments are also available.

Many tours feature a visit to the Blue Lagoon, but if you're traveling independently, it makes sense to visit right after you fly in or before you head home, as it's very close to Keflavík airport. A rejuvenating soak is a great way to kick off your trip or end it on a relaxing note.

The entrance fee is 6,000ISK for adults, 3,000ISK for teenagers, 3,000ISK for senior citizens, and children under the age of 13 are admitted free. Because of the increase in tourism over the past few years, the Blue Lagoon now requires that you book a time slot ahead of your arrival. Thousands of people visit the site every day, and it could be quite crowded during summer months. If you don't bring your own towel, you can rent one at the front desk, along with swimsuits and bathing caps.

SALTFISKSETUR (SALTFISH MUSEUM)

The **Saltfish Museum** (Hafnargata 12A, tel. 354/420-1190, www.saltfisksetur.is, 9am-6pm daily, entrance 500ISK) is a museum that tells you exactly what Iceland's fish trade was like from 1770 to 1965, when saltfish ceased to be Iceland's top export. Photos, fishing equipment, and even a full-size fishing boat from the early 20th century are on display, explaining the importance of saltfish to Iceland, economically and culturally. If you're curious about the region, would like to learn more about processing saltfish in the olden days, or would like to get a look at an old-school fishing boat, be sure to stop by.

FISHERMEN MEMORIAL

A sad part of Iceland's fishing history is the stories of men that went out to sea to never return. There's a moving memorial in downtown Grindavík, in the main garden near the Saltfish Museum, showing a mother with her son and daughter waiting for their fisherman husband/father to return home from sea. It's a reminder that the fish used for consumption and trade has come at a high price for many families over the years. The memorial was created by sculptor Ragnar Kjartansson.

Sports and Recreation
BIKING

Reykjanes has several well-maintained trails perfect for cycling. **Arctic Adventures** (tel. 354/562-7000, www.adventures.is) operates a popular mountain biking tour that departs from Reykjavík by bus. Biking begins at the Blue Lagoon. The easy bike ride takes tourists on trails that run along volcanic craters, rugged lava fields, and bubbling hot springs throughout the peninsula. The tour runs mid-May-mid-September for 33,000ISK and ends with a dip in the soothing, geothermally heated water at the Blue Lagoon.

CAMPING

Tourists can camp from mid-May to mid-September at Grindavík's Campsite (Austurvegur 26, tel. 354/660-7323, 1,200ISK) by the harbor. A popular campsite, Grindavík's location offers laundry facilities, a common eating area, and a playground for children that has swings and a spider net for climbing. The campsite accommodates tents, RVs, and campers, with access to hookups. The grassy field is an open space with beautiful views of mountains. There's also a paved entrance to the campsite and a large parking area. Close by is an area to empty camper port-a-potties.

GOLF

Just four kilometers southwest from the Blue Lagoon, Húsatóftir Golf Course (Húsatóftum, tel. 354/426-8720, paller@grindavik.is, 5,000ISK) is an 18-hole golf course where visitors can golf from late May to early September, depending on the weather. The course sits on a scenic part of the southern part of the country with picturesque views of the landscape. However, the course can be busy with locals during the high season of June-July. Be sure to call ahead for a tee time.

SWIMMING

Grindavík is home to one of the best pools in South Iceland. The Grindavík Swimming Pool (Austurvegur 1, tel. 354/426-7555, www.grindavik.is, 7am-8pm Mon.-Fri., 10am-5pm Sat.-Sun. June-Aug., 400ISK) has a 25-meter pool, hot tubs, tanning beds, a water slide, children's pool, and fitness center.

Accommodations

The ★ Blue Lagoon Clinic (Svartsengi, tel. 354/420-8806, www.bluelagoon.com/Clinic, doubles from 46,000ISK) is a luxurious hotel connected to the Blue Lagoon specializing in treating psoriasis and eczema. Guests travel to the healing waters from around the world in the hope of treating skin diseases through specialized treatments. The clinic has 15 rooms that offer comfortable beds, modern decor, and beautiful views of the lagoon. To stay at the clinic, guests must have a form completed by a dermatologist citing that you have a form of psoriasis or eczema.

Open all year long, Guesthouse Borg (Boragarhraun 2, tel. 354/895-8686, www.guesthouseborg.com, rooms from 14,000ISK) is a basic, no-frills guesthouse in the center of Grindavík. The seven-room guesthouse has shared kitchen facilities, bathrooms, and washing machines, and is a five-minute drive from the Blue Lagoon. It's a clean and comfortable place to stay, but nothing to write home about.

The 32-room guesthouse **Northern Light Inn** (Grindavíkurvegur 1, tel. 354/426-8650, www.nli.is, doubles from 34,500ISK) offers cozy, bright, rooms with free Wi-Fi, satellite TV, and stunning views. An in-house restaurant offers classic Icelandic fare with plenty of fish and lamb dishes as well as a couple of vegetarian options. A conference area attracts business travelers, but the proximity to the Blue Lagoon is a big draw for tourists.

Food

Bryggjan (Miðgarður 2, tel. 354/426-7100, www.kaffibryggjan.is, 11am-6pm daily, 600ISK) is Grindavík's main coffee house and a favorite among locals and tourists alike. The cozy eatery is light on decor but known for its light meals, sandwiches, and soups. The lobster soup is delicious and affordable at just 600ISK.

The ★ **Lava Blue Lagoon Restaurant** (Svartsengi, tel. 354/420-8800, www.bluelagoon.com, noon-8:30 pm daily, entrées from 5,900ISK) is very much a spa restaurant; ingredients are fresh and local, and the recipes are healthy. You will find fresh vegetables and fish as well as lean meats. The menu accommodates a host of dietary requirements. You will dine in a minimalist atmosphere with cool hues and modern accents.

Mamma Mía (Víkurbraut 31, tel. 354/426-7860, 5pm-10pm Mon.-Thurs., 11:30am-11:30pm Fri.-Sun., entrées from 1,400ISK) is Grindavík's only pizzeria. It serves up classics like margherita and pepperoni but also does some specialty pies with interesting ingredients, including tuna fish and pineapple. Hamburgers, sandwiches, and salads are also available. It's a family-friendly restaurant, one that locals and their kids frequent often. You can eat in or do takeaway.

★ **Salthúsið** (Stamphólsvegur 9, tel. 354/426-9700, www.salthusid.is, noon-10pm daily mid-May-mid-Sept., entrées from 2,400ISK), or "The Salt House," is a favorite among local fishers, residents, and tourists. There's a lot of saltfish on the menu, but guests can also choose from lamb and chicken dishes, as well as burgers, sandwiches, and fish-and-chips from this quiet eatery. The garlic-roasted lobster with salad and garlic bread is delicious. If you have room, be sure to check out the decadent dessert menu, which includes deep-fried bananas with vanilla ice cream and caramel sauce, and French chocolate cake with fresh cream.

Information and Services

The tourist information center is located in the **Saltfish Museum** (Hafnargata 12A, tel. 354/420-1190, 10am-5pm daily). The gas station N1 and grocery chain Netto are situated downtown on Víkurbraut.

Getting There and Around

By car, Grindavík is 50 kilometers from Reykjavík. Drivers should take Route 41 west to Route 43 south. It's about a 40-minute drive.

There are three daily departures from BSÍ bus station (www.bsi.is) in Reykjavík to Grindavík all year-round from the company **Reykjavík**

Excursions (tel. 354/580-5400, www.re.is) for 3,900ISK. There are return buses to Reykjavík as well. The buses go to the Blue Lagoon as well as the center of Grindavík (about 1.25 hours).

KRÝSUVÍK

The Krýsuvík geothermal area, which is 35 kilometers south of Reykjavík, is popular among geology buffs and hikers. Gurgling mud pools amid the yellow, red, and orange clay-like earth are intertwined with dancing steam and hot springs. The many hiking paths allow you to feel lost in the outer space-like atmosphere. The region gives you a great sense of Iceland's raw, natural geothermal energy, which powers much of the island. Take some time to roam, but be sure to stay within the designated roped-off areas to avoid getting burned by spray and steam. To get to the region, take Route 42 from Reykjavík. It's about a 40-minute drive.

the geothermal area of Krýsuvík

The Golden Circle

If you ask an Icelander which tour you should take if you want a taste of Iceland outside of Reykjavík, you will most likely hear the "Golden Circle" tour. Encompassing the three most commonly visited sights in South Iceland, the Golden Circle gives you a slice of Icelandic history at Þingvellir, a view of Iceland's bubbling geothermal activity at Geysir, and a peek of a roaring, powerful waterfall at Gullfoss. The sights are classically Icelandic, and postcard perfect, whether in summer or winter. Because of the popularity of the sights, it's pretty easy to get there. You can pre-book a tour through many tourism companies, or simply go to Reykjavík's main bus terminal, BSÍ (Vatnsmýrarvegur 10, Reykjavík, tel. 354/562-1011, www.bsi.is), and buy a same-day ticket through Reykjavík Excursions (tel. 354/580-5400, www.re.is) for 9,500ISK for an eight-hour tour. If you want to rent a car and view the sights independently, take Route 1 past the town of Selfoss, then Route 30 to Gullfoss, then Route 35 to Geysir, and Routes 37, 365, and 36 to Þingvellir. In total, the Golden Circle is a 300-kilometer circular route, leaving from and returning to Reykjavík.

ÞINGVELLIR NATIONAL PARK

The birth of Iceland as a nation began at Þingvellir. Literally translated to "Parliament Plains," Þingvellir is the site of Iceland's first general assembly, which was said to be established in the year 930, and the meeting place of the Icelandic parliament until 1798. Many significant sights are at Þingvellir, including Almannagjá (All Man's Gorge) and Lögberg (Law Rock). Icelanders made sure that Þingvellir is a protected national park by establishing it as such in 1930.

Visitors also come to the area for its geological significance, as it is the site of a rift valley that marks the crest of the Mid-Atlantic Ridge and is home to Þingvallavatn, the largest natural lake on the island, which has a surface area of 84 square kilometers.

Sights

ÞINGVELLIR INTERPRETIVE CENTER

The Þingvellir Interpretive Center (tel. 354/482-2660, www.thingvellir. is, 9am-5pm daily year-round, free) gives a great overview of the national park, its history, and its geological significance. Stop in to see the interactive display and then pick up hiking maps at the information center next door.

ALMANNAGJÁ

The moss-covered, stony landscape is home to Almannagjá (All Man's Gorge), which is the tallest cliff face and the original backdrop to the Alþing. This rock structure is considered the edge of the North American plate, which visitors can get a look at up close. It's an impressive sight, so be sure you have your camera ready.

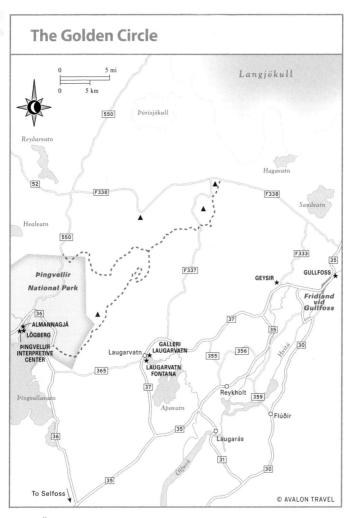

LÖGBERG (LAW ROCK)

Lögberg (Law Rock) is a popular site within the park. Iceland's Commonwealth period ran from 930 till 1262, and during that time, the Law Rock was the center of the Alþing (parliament). A man known as the "law speaker" proclaimed the laws of the Commonwealth, was required to memorize the laws, and had three years to recite all of them. At the Law Rock, members of the Alþing gave speeches and held significant events, including where the calendar was confirmed for the year as well as legal rulings. It's where Icelandic democracy began.

The Öxará (Axe) River flows over seemingly endless lava fields, emitting a haunting mist in the winter months. It's serene and eerie until it reaches the waterfall Öxaráfoss, where the water tumbles and roars over the cliffs. At the river's edge, visitors can see a church and farmhouse, which is the official summer residence of Iceland's prime minister. The church, Þingvallakirkja, is a charming wood church in traditional Icelandic design that dates from 1859. Tourists can visit the church 9am-5pm daily from mid-May to early September. Visitors can go inside, take photos, and sit on a pew and reflect. The interior features a wooden pulpit and bells from earlier churches. There's a small cemetery behind the church where celebrated poets Einar Benediktsson and Jonasa Hallgrimsson are buried.

Sports and Recreation
DIVING

Scuba diving in the naturally filtered, pure water of Þingvallavatn lake is sublime. While some may think that diving in Iceland sounds strange, a growing number of tourists are opting to take a dip and check out what lies within the clear lake. Surveying the underwater basalt walls, multicolored algae, and sloping sands is magical. Don't even think about going in without a drysuit, as the water temperature hovers around 3°C (37°F). Diving is possible year-round, and day tours start at 35,000ISK. There are rules to obey, so don't attempt to dive without a guide. **Dive Iceland** (Ásbúðartröð 17, Hafnarfjörður, tel. 354/699-3000, www.dive.is) offers a two-tank dive package for about 35,000ISK.

FISHING

Boats are not allowed on the lake, but fishing permits are sold at the information center. Tourists have a chance of catching arctic char and brown

Þingvellir National Park

trout. Be sure to obey the rules and pay for the permit. The fishing season at the lake runs from May 1 to September 15, and permits are about 30,000ISK.

HIKING

Þingvellir is lovely for the casual hiker. Acres of flat lava fields make it an easy hike, but be sure to be careful of open rock fissures along the way, because you could fall in. There are scores of foot trails and plenty of interesting rock formations and rugged landscape to see. You can get information about trails and the surrounding area at the visitors center. If you're looking to scale some small mountains, check out **Mount Syðstasúla** (1,085 meters), which is in the northern region of the park and is the easiest to climb. The view from the top is spectacular.

HORSE RIDING

Þingvellir is a popular spot for riding horses, with several trails that offer the chance to check out some of the more beautiful and geologically significant areas of the park. Most tours cost about 12,500ISK and last for 3-4 hours. Seeing the region by horseback is a beautiful way to survey the land. **Reykjavík Excursions** (tel. 354/580-5400, www.re.is) offers a horse-riding day tour in Þingvellir for 19,900ISK.

Accommodations and Food

Þingvellir National Park's only hotel, Valholl Hotel, unfortunately burned down in 2009. However, there are hotels to stay at in nearby Laugarvatn and Selfoss. If you would like to stay within the park limits, your only option is camping at one of Þingvellir's five campgrounds in two sections of the park: at the Leirar section of the park, which is a five-minute walk from the Þingvellir information center, and in Vatnskot section, which is by Lake Þingvallavatn. The Leirar campground is divided into four campsites: Fagrabrekka, Syðri-Leirar, Hvannabrekka, and Nyrðri-Leirar. The Vatnskot campground is situated at an abandoned farm by the lake. All campsites have access to toilets, electricity, and cooking facilities. The difference in the two sections is not about amenities, but whether you want to camp close to the lake or stay closer to the information center. Both sections have great landscape views and spacious fields. The campgrounds are open June 1-Septembter 1, and it costs 1,300ISK per person.

Information and Services

The **tourist information center** (tel. 354/482-2660, www.thingvellir.is, 9am-7pm daily May-Oct., 9am-5pm daily Nov.-Apr.) is next to the main campground.

Getting There and Around

Þingvellir is 46 kilometers northeast of Reykjavík. By car, take Route 36, which will take you to the northern part of the park.

While there is no public transportation available to get to the park, a number of tours include a stop at Þingvellir. Check out Reykjavík Excursions (tel. 354/580-5400, www.re.is) for daily departures.

LAUGARVATN

Laugarvatn, or "Bathing Waters," is a lake situated between Þingvellir and the geothermal hot spot of Geysir. Historically, members of Iceland's parliament (Alþing) visited the springs due to the proximity to where parliament met at Þingvellir for hundreds of years. The lake's water temperature hovers around 104°F, making it a unique and warm swimming experience.

Sights
GALLERI LAUGARVATN

When not enjoying the soothing hot springs or vast landscape, steal away for a few minutes at Galleri Laugarvatn (Haholt 1, tel. 354/486-1016, www.gallerilaugarvatn.is, 1pm-5pm daily), a charming little gallery that features local handicrafts, ranging from glass tea light holders to unique paper crafts.

LAUGARVATN FONTANA

The Laugarvatn Fontana (Hverabraut 1, tel. 354/486-1400, www.fontana. is, 11am-9pm daily, 3,200ISK entry fee) is worth a stop before or after you visit geothermal hot spot Geysir. The facility's sauna captures the steam just as it escapes from the earth. Tourists and locals can be seen basking in the natural sauna and hot springs, enjoying the geothermal energy up close and personal. For something really unique to the region, each day at 2:30pm there is a planned walk to the on-site geothermal bakery from the reception area. Visitors can experience the geothermal bakery first-hand and see as the staff digs out rye bread that has been buried in the ground, left to bake naturally from the geothermally heated earth. After the walk, you can try the bread, served hot from the ground with some butter. It's delicious!

Sports and Recreation
SWIMMING

Situated downtown, the Laugarvatn Swimming Pool (Hverabraut 2, tel. 354/486-1251, 10am-10pm Mon.-Fri., 10am-6pm Sat.-Sun. June-mid-Aug., 5pm-8pm Mon., Wed., and Fri., 1pm-5pm Sat. mid-Aug.-May, 500ISK) is popular among locals, but it's a nice break from the summer tourist rush at the Fontana spa nearby. Head here if you would like a quiet spot to take a dip.

Accommodations

Location is key for Hótel Edda ML Laugarvatn (Skólatún, tel.

354/444-4810, www.hoteledda.is, mid-June-mid-Aug., rooms from 11,100ISK), as this 101-room hotel is a popular stop for those touring the Golden Circle. Rooms are basic and no-frills, with double beds, IKEA-style furniture, and crisp white bedding. Thirty-two rooms have private bathrooms, while the rest share facilities, and there is free Wi-Fi in common areas. Guests get a 10 percent discount for the geothermal steam baths at the nearby Fontana spa.

Efstidalur II (Bláskógabyggð, tel. 354/486-1186, www.efstidalur.is, rooms from 14,000ISK) is a charming farmhouse bed-and-breakfast with an in-house restaurant, friendly staff, and horse rentals. Situated close to the Fontana spa, the B&B is also in the proximity of the Golden Circle.

One of the busiest hostels in South Iceland, Laugarvatn Youth Hostel (Dalsel, tel. 354/486-1215, www.laugarvatnhostel.is, open all year, double rooms from 10,900ISK) sleeps 140 people in single, double, and family rooms. Ten rooms have private bathroom facilities, while the rest share. Kitchen and laundry facilities are available, and the staff is very warm and helpful. There's also a big hot tub on the property.

Food

At Restaurant Linden (Lindarbraut 2, tel. 354/486-1262, www.laugarvatn. is, noon-10pm daily in summer, entrées from 1,800ISK), owner and head chef Baldur Öxdal Halldórsson has created an upscale, fine dining experience in a town with fewer than 300 residents. Guests have a lot of choices, from Icelandic mainstays to more exotic fare, with dishes ranging from reindeer meat burgers and pan-fried arctic char to tender lamb filets and smoked cod. The classic decor and friendly staff make this little restaurant a treasure. You won't find typical tourist fare here.

Getting There and Around

Laugarvatn is just 77 kilometers northeast from Reykjavík and is easily accessible by car and bus. If driving, take Route 37, which heads toward Gullfoss and Geysir. Turn off on Route 354, which will take you to Laugarvatn.

The Strætó bus company (tel. 354/540-2700, www.straeto.is) has one daily departure to Laugarvatn year-round, leaving from the Mjodd bus terminal (tel. 354/587-0230) in Reykjavík. The trip is about 2.5 hours, and it costs 1,400ISK.

GEYSIR

Iceland's geysers are the most obvious demonstration of the island's natural geothermal energy. A bubbling pool of hot water in clay-like earth erupts into a mountain of steam, delighting spectators.

Historically, Geysir is the most famous of Iceland's geysers; it's actually the source of the word "geyser." Geologists theorized that in the 13th century earthquakes stirred the underground workings of the natural hot springs, causing them to gush, releasing pressure, steam, and water up to 20 meters into the air.

Visitors to the site today aren't going to see Geysir erupt, as the geyser hasn't blown since 2005; it's been rendered dormant. But don't fret, because Geysir's nearby cousin, **Strokkur** (Churn), erupts every seven minutes or so, delighting tourists. The churning, gurgling pool of water turning out a rush of pressure is an impressive sight. Be sure to have your camera ready.

Crowds gather at Strokkur to watch the frequent eruptions. Please be careful and stay behind the ropes or you may get hit with hot spray.

After walking around the geothermal area, stop at the **visitors center** (10am-5pm May-Aug., noon-4pm Jan.-Apr. and Sept.-Dec.). It has a short multimedia exhibition about the geology of the region, a small café serving refreshments, and a souvenir shop.

Sports and Recreation
CAMPING
About 100 meters from the Geysir area is a **campground** (tel. 354/480-6800, 1,000ISK) that has hot showers, pool access, and a common barbecue area. Hótel Geysir operates the campsite, and you pay at the Geysir Shops just across from the campgrounds. For an additional 500ISK you can have access to electricity, and the use of the swimming pool and hot tub at Hótel Geysir will run you an additional 500ISK.

Accommodations and Food
You can't stay any closer to the geysers than at the **Hótel Geysir** (Geysir, tel. 354/480-6800, www.geysircenter.is, rooms from 18,000ISK). The property features posh suites that have huge Jacuzzi tubs and luxurious beds right across the way from the geysers. Guests can also stay in chalets on the property that are essentially double rooms. The decor is a bit rustic, but

the Strokkur geyser erupting

the rooms are comfortable. Visitors have access to an outdoor swimming pool and hot tub, and the geysers are just two minutes away. The in-house restaurant (8am-10pm daily) serves up delicious dishes ranging from fresh Icelandic cod to lamb and beef entrées. A lunch buffet is popular among tourists. A three-course dinner menu will run you about 7,000ISK.

Guesthouse Geysir (Haukadalur, tel. 354/486-8733, www.geysirgolf.is, double rooms from 16,000ISK) doesn't have the perks of the Hótel Geysir, but the guesthouse has single, double, and triple rooms, as well as sleeping bag accommodations and free breakfast in the summer months. Guests also have access to a kitchen to prepare and store their food. The guesthouse is next to a nine-hole golf course. It's clean and comfortable and adequate for a quick stay.

Getting There and Around

Geysir is about a 1.5-hour drive east from Reykjavík. You start out on Route 1, then take Route 35, which takes you directly to the site.

SBA-Norðurleið bus service (tel. 354/550-0770, www.sba.is) passes by Geysir daily during its highland route toward Akureyri. You can request a stop at the site. The ride from Reykjavík is about 2.5 hours (4,600ISK). The bus runs during the summer only.

GULLFOSS

The thundering, roaring waterfall of Gullfoss epitomizes the raw beauty of Iceland. Gullfoss (Golden Falls) tumbles into the Hvíta (White) River, which is a perfect name given the turbulent white water. There are three levels of water at the falls, ranging from 11 meters to 21 meters, meeting at a 70-meter gorge. If you get too close, expect to get soaked.

Because of Iceland's changing weather, you have a good chance to see a rainbow over the falls, making for a perfect snapshot of your visit. Plan to walk around the site, enjoying not only the wonder of the falls, but also

Gullfoss

the beautiful surrounding landscape. In the summer, there are miles of lush green grass and frequent rainbows on sunny/rainy days. Be careful; it could be slippery.

No matter what time of year, there are scores of tour buses and independent drivers visiting the falls, and that's for a very good reason. It's gorgeous.

There is currently a fight between landowners and the Icelandic government over whether to charge visitors a fee to visit the falls. At the time of writing, it was undecided and still in the courts.

An on-site café includes a souvenir shop and offers some brochures about the surrounding area.

Accommodations and Food

A short walking distance from the falls and parking area, Gullfosskaffi (Gullfoss Café) (tel. 354/486-6500, www.gullfoss.is, 9am-9:30pm daily, entrées from 1,200ISK) is the place to go when you're in the area. The Icelandic lamb meat soup on the menu is a winner, and a favorite among visitors, but sandwiches, cakes, and coffee are also available.

Hótel Gullfoss (Brattholt, tel. 354/486-8979, www.hotelgullfoss.is, rooms from 21,000ISK) is situated perfectly, just three kilometers from the falls in a remote area. The resort-like atmosphere is comfortable and a great place to spend the night while touring the Golden Circle. Every room has a private bathroom and is classically furnished with comfortable beds. An in-house restaurant and hot tub out back make for a comfortable stay.

Getting There and Around

By car, Gullfoss is 115 kilometers northeast from Reykjavík. The drive takes about 1.5 hours on Route 35.

If you plan to travel by bus, SBA-Norðurleið (tel. 354/550-0770, www.sba.is) makes one daily stop to and from Gullfoss on its Kjölur (Highlands) route. The ride from Reykjavík is about 3.25 hours (4,800ISK). The bus runs during the summer only.

Background

The Landscape 86

History 89

Government and Economy 91

People and Culture 93

The Landscape

GEOGRAPHY

Iceland is the westernmost European country, situated in the North Atlantic between North America and Europe. Iceland is east of Greenland and south of the Arctic Circle, atop the northern Mid-Atlantic Ridge. It lies 859 kilometers from Scotland and 4,200 kilometers from New York City. The area of Iceland is 103,022 square kilometers, and a frequent comparison among Icelandic tour guides is that Iceland is roughly the size of the U.S. state Kentucky.

Climate

Iceland isn't as cold as you may think. The Gulf Stream swirls along the western and southern coasts and works to moderate Iceland's climate. But moderate doesn't mean calm, as the Gulf Stream is responsible for the frequent weather changes—as in lots of wind and rain. The biggest climate challenge is the unpredictability of it. The "summer" tourist season runs from the end of May to the beginning of September, and during that time, the climate ranges from rainy May days to the midnight sun in July to the possibility of snow in September. The winter climate brings colder temperatures, dark days, whipping winds, and the possibility of seeing northern lights flicker and dance on clear nights.

Weather

Weather in Iceland is not casual conversation, but serious business. Weather forecasts are frequent but largely hit or miss. The weather can change rapidly, from calm winds and sunny skies to rain, snow, sleet and back to calm wind and sunny skies, all in the same hour. It's unpredictable, frustrating, exhilarating, and confusing for many tourists, but Icelanders have learned to adapt and go with the flow. As a result, plans tend to be loose, whether it's for meeting friends for coffee or a job interview. If the weather acts up, locals understand.

Some of the most extreme weather you could experience on this island is wind—the type of wind in winter that could knock you off your feet. If the weather forecast is showing strong winds, especially in the countryside, alter your plans accordingly. Do not underestimate the wind, and heed any storm advisories. Be safe, smart, and prepared. The changing conditions are part of the experience of traveling to Iceland, and the key is being prepared with layers of clothing, proper footwear, and waterproof outerwear.

Previous: statue of Leifur Eiríksson; pink bicycle gate.

Geology

Iceland is a volcanic island constantly in flux, with magma breaking through fissures and periodic eruptions that redesign the rocky landscape. Iceland's land is made up of igneous rock, most of which is basalt, which forms from cooling magma. Most of Iceland's mountains were formed with basalt that has been carved by water and ice erosion. Earthquakes are a common occurrence, but tremors are rarely felt. At the time of this writing, a volcanic fissure eruption in Holuhraun has been ongoing for weeks, and there have been up to 1,000 tremors near the region per day.

VOLCANOES

Volcanic eruptions are a growing source of tourism for the country. Local travel companies offer helicopter, jeep and airplane tours when an eruption occurs. Most of Iceland's volcanic eruptions are fissure vents, like the 2014 Holuhraun eruption, where lava seeps out of the cracks in the earth's crust. Holuhraun produced fountains of lava shooting out of the earth, delighting photographers and keeping volcanologists busy trying to determine if the nearby Bárðarbunga volcano will erupt. At the time of this writing, it hasn't. The three most active volcanoes on the island are Katla, Hekla, and Eyjafjallajökull. Eyjafjallajökull erupted in 2010, grounding air travel in Europe for days thanks to a large ash cloud.

Residents have learned to adapt to eruptions, and most volcanoes are away from residential areas. In the case of the 2014 Holuhraun eruption, the surrounding area near Vatnajökull was evacuated of locals, and tourists and animals were moved from the area. The main threat was toxins in the air, and those close to the region were asked to stay indoors and turn up their heating if they were sensitive to air quality.

Air

When there isn't an eruption, Iceland's air is some of the cleanest and purest

Eyjafjallajökull eruption in 2010

BACKGROUND THE LANDSCAPE

you will experience, as pollution is low and the Gulf Stream produces a strong, steady wind that blows toxins away. The main source of pollution on the island is from industry, mainly aluminum smelters.

Water

Like the air, Iceland's water is perfectly pure. There's clean, tasty drinking water on tap and geothermally heated water that powers swimming pools and hot water in homes. Snow can fall in any month of the year, but large snowfalls are uncommon in the Reykjavík area, at least during the last couple of decades. Ice covers about 11 percent of the country, mostly in the form of Iceland's largest glaciers: Vatnajökull, Hofsjökull, Langjökull, and Mýrdalsjökull. Melting ice from the glaciers and melting snow form the rivers.

Iceland's water also serves as some of its tourist attractions. The man-made Blue Lagoon near Grindavík allows visitors to bathe in geothermally heated water, which soothes and heals the skin. Locals and tourists enjoy hot springs throughout the country, and spectacular waterfalls with roaring water tumble over basalt rock and earth. The largest and most visited waterfalls in Iceland are Gullfoss, Dettifoss, Goðafoss, and Skógafoss.

Northern Lights

The biggest winter attraction in Iceland is the aurora borealis (northern lights). People travel from around the world to catch a glimpse of the green, white, blue, and red lights dancing in the night sky. There's something very special about bundling up in your warmest winter gear, trekking outside main towns to avoid bright lights, and hunting for the aurora borealis. The phenomenon is caused by solar winds, which push electronic particles to collide with molecules of atmospheric gases, causing an emission of bright light. The best time to see northern lights is from October to March, and there are forecasts predicting visibility on the **national weather website**

the northern lights above a lighthouse on the Reykjanes Peninsula (www.vedur.is). When the forecast is strong, it's best to drive (or take a tour bus) to a dark area and look up. Northern lights tours are offered by Reykjavik Excursions (www.re.is).

History

SETTLEMENT

Iceland has the distinction of being the last country in Europe to be settled. The country is known for impeccable record-keeping, and for that reason, it's known that the first permanent resident in Iceland was Ingólfur Arnarson, who built a farm in Reykjavík in the year 874. The earliest settlers were emigrants from Norway who opposed the king, Harald, due to a blood feud, and they wanted to make a new life in a new land. In addition to the Norwegians, their slaves from Ireland and Scotland were brought along as well, which means Icelanders are a blend of Norse and Celtic stock.

As word got out about the new land, within a few decades most of the coastline was claimed, with farms and fishing stations popping up. A government wasn't formed until 930, when the Alþing (parliament) was created, but the new settlers in the meantime opted for each farmstead to have a self-appointed chief. Once the Alþing was established in Þingvellir, a legislative body was elected.

CONVERSION TO CHRISTIANITY

Christianity came to Iceland, some say, by force. By the 10th century, there was mounting political pressure from the king of Norway to convert to Christianity or face the consequences, which would be war. As the end of the first millennium grew near, many prominent Icelanders had accepted the new faith.

By the year 1000, the Alþing was divided into two religious groups: modern Christians and pagans. The two groups were steadfast in their beliefs, and a civil war seemed likely. The law speaker, Þorgeir Þorkelsson, was called upon for a decision. (The law speaker was appointed to office and was required to recite the law during parliamentary meetings.) Þorgeir decided that Iceland would be a Christian country, but that pagans could still celebrate their rituals in the privacy of their farms. Þorgeir was baptized in Þingvellir, and Christianity became the law of the land. Christian churches were built, a bishop was established in 1056, and the majority of Icelanders remain Christian today.

DANISH RULE

Iceland remained under Norwegian kingship rule until 1380, when the death of Olav IV put an end to the Norwegian male royal line. Norway (and by extension Iceland) became part of the Kalmar Union, along with Denmark and Sweden, with Denmark as the dominant nation. At this time,

Iceland became effectively a colony of Denmark, with the king owning the land and the church's money. Iceland's government now answered to Denmark and did so for the next several hundred years.

Iceland was still very much centered on fishing and farming, and it was quite isolated from the dealings in mainland Europe. In 1602, the Danish government, which was pursuing mercantilist policies, ordered that Iceland was forbidden to trade with countries other than Denmark. The Danish trade monopoly would remain in effect until 1786.

INDEPENDENCE

Iceland began inching toward independence when it was granted a Minister of Icelandic Affairs in 1904, who would be based in Reykjavík. Hannes Hafstein was the first to serve in the minister position, and his place in Iceland's history is prominent. During this time, Iceland became more autonomous, building up Reykjavík's harbor, founding the University of Iceland, and eventually creating its own flag in 1915.

Over the next couple of decades, Iceland was taking more control of its affairs, and when World War II started, there was an economic opportunity for Iceland. Iceland was invited to join the Allied war effort by Great Britain, but Iceland's government refused, declaring its neutrality. Britain pushed for Iceland's cooperation, but ultimately British naval forces arrived in Iceland, began building a base near Keflavík, and occupied the country for its proximity to North America. In all, 25,000 British soldiers occupied Iceland, which created a significant number of jobs for Icelanders. The British left in 1941, but more than 40,000 American troops replaced them, continuing the economic win for Iceland. There were jobs, opportunity, an American radio station, and lots of money flowing into the tiny island nation.

Denmark took a step back from Iceland's affairs during World War II, and Icelanders eventually held a referendum on its independence. Almost 99 percent of the population voted in the referendum, 97 percent of which voted for independence. On June 17, 1944, Iceland became totally independent of Denmark. American troops maintained the Keflavík NATO base until 2006.

MODERN-DAY ICELAND

Iceland plodded along, building up its fishing resources, investing in infrastructure, and looking toward the future. During years of rule by the center-right Independence Party, banks were deregulated in the early 2000s and Iceland's financial sector began taking off at a rapid pace. Iceland was being lauded for its financial acumen, but it all imploded in 2008, when the country's three major banks failed, sending Iceland into one of the deepest financial crises in modern-day Europe. Today, Iceland is still rebuilding and is recovering.

One of the most divisive issues in Iceland has been whether to join the European Union (EU). Polls indicate that the majority of Icelanders are against joining, and the Independence/Progressive coalition that was elected in 2013 halted EU talks altogether. The debate continues to rage on as Icelanders demand a referendum on the matter, which was promised by the parties in power. It will be interesting to see how this plays out going forward.

Iceland today is reaping the benefits of increased tourism. People from around the world have become aware of and infatuated with Iceland for its raw nature, volcanic eruptions, and culture.

Government and Economy

GOVERNMENT

Iceland's government dates back to the year 930, when the Alþing (parliament) was formed, but its constitution was signed on June 17, 1944, when Iceland achieved independence from Denmark. The Alþing, which consists of 63 seats, meets four days a week near Austurvollur in the center of Reykjavík. Nine judges make up the High Court of Iceland and are appointed by the president. Iceland's president serves more of a ceremonial role, while the prime minister holds most of the executive powers. Other high-level cabinet positions are the Minister of Finance and Minister of Foreign Affairs.

Political Parties

Iceland's political party system is in double digits, with 13 main parties running for seats in the 2013 election. However, in the Alþing, six parties hold seats: Independence Party, Progressive Party, Social Democratic Alliance, Left-Green Movement, Bright Future, and the Pirate Party.

The Progressive Party (Framsóknarflokkurinn) is a center-right party that was formed to protect the interests of fishers and farmers. The current prime minister, Sigmundur Davið Gunnlaugsson, a former journalist, has served as leader of the Progressives since 2009. The Independence Party (Sjálfstadisflokkurinn), the second largest party in the country, was in power in the years leading up to the economic collapse of 2008. They were voted out of the majority in 2009 but regained seats, and power, in 2013. The Social Democratic Alliance, Bright Future, Left-Green Movement, and Pirate Party represent the more liberal political parties on the island. The sitting president, Ólafur Ragnar Grímsson, was a member of the now-defunct People's Alliance, and is known for having more liberal/moderate views. He was elected to a fifth term in 2012 and has stated that he will not be running for reelection.

Defense

Iceland does not have a military, but it hosted British and American troops in Keflavík during and after World War II. American troops remained in

Iceland, on the NATO base, until 2006, at the height of the U.S. wars in Iraq and Afghanistan. Iceland's Coast Guard oversees crisis management and protection along the coasts of Iceland and has been known to participate in daring rescues at sea. The Icelandic police force consists of fewer than 1,000 police officers, who maintain the peace. The crime rate is exceptionally low in Iceland, and police officers do not carry handguns.

ECONOMY

Iceland's economy is best known to tourists for taking a dive during the 2008 financial crisis. The island is still recovering from the collapse, and tourism is playing a large role in that recovery, along with alternative energy.

Banking Crisis

In early 2008, Iceland's currency began to take a dive compared to the euro, and that was the first international signal that there was deep trouble lurking in Iceland's financial sector. By the autumn, all three of Iceland's major banks had failed, lifting the veil on Iceland's house of cards. Following the collapse, unemployment soared, pension funds shrank, and inflation skyrocketed to more than 70 percent. Loans taken out in foreign currency became unmanageable to thousands of Icelanders, credit lines were cut off, and capital controls were put in place that restricted how much money Icelanders could move out of the country. It was dire. The IMF made an emergency loan of $2.1 billion in November 2008, and the country started to look to rebuild and recover.

Tourism

An increase in tourism made strides in Iceland recovering. In fact, the increase makes tourism the second-biggest revenue source after fish. In 2014, tourism agencies in Iceland predicted that one million tourists would land in Iceland, which is more than triple Iceland's population. Most of Iceland's tourists come from the United States, Great Britain, the Nordic countries, Germany, France, and Switzerland. Tourism is also increasing from Asian tourists. The issue going forward is how to keep tourism sustainable and to protect Iceland's land from too much traffic.

Fishing

It's no secret that fish are the lifeblood of Iceland. They nourish its residents and are Iceland's number one export. Iceland's biggest trading partners are within the European Union, which is interesting because the opposition to joining the EU, for many, is for Iceland to maintain complete control of its fishing stock. Cod is the most common fish export.

Energy

One of the perks of living on a volcanic island is having a hotbed of geothermal energy. About 98 percent of the island's energy comes from geothermal and hydroelectric sources, which accounts for low cost and low pollution. However, the pollution that does inhabit Iceland's airspace stems from an increasing number of aluminum smelters that have popped up in the last couple of decades. Foreign aluminum providers look to Iceland for its cheap energy and vast land. It's a trade-off that many Icelanders remain unhappy about, while the smelters do create jobs and revenue for the country. As of this writing, Iceland was in talks with the United Kingdom on how to export geothermal energy there.

Currency

Iceland maintains its own currency, as it is not a member of the European Union. The Icelandic króna has a small circulation and is pegged to the euro. Following the financial crisis, inflation soared more than 70 percent, and Iceland's currency took a dive. The uncertainty was a maddening time for many Icelanders. Inflation is still high, and exchange rates rise and fall. Capital controls were created in 2008 that limit how much money Icelanders can move out of the country, and they remain in place. If an Icelander is traveling abroad and wants foreign currency, they must present their plane ticket at their bank to receive foreign currency. Life has changed since 2008.

People and Culture

POPULATION

Nearly 330,000 people call Iceland home, and more than two-thirds live in the capital city, Reykjavík, and its outlying suburbs. Outside of Reykjavík, Hafnarfjörður, and Kopavogur, the most populated towns in Iceland include Keflavík and Selfoss in the south, Akureyri in the north, Akranes and Isafjörður in the west, and Höfn and Egilsstaðir in the east. More than 90 percent of the island population is composed of native Icelanders, but the foreign-born population continues to grow with migrant workers and refugees. Iceland is as multicultural today as it has ever been.

Native Icelanders have a genetic makeup that combines Gaelic and Norse heritage, and many Icelanders consider themselves Nordic instead of Scandinavian. Social lives center around family, as Icelanders tend to be a close-knit bunch. People tend to either know one another or have friends in common.

LANGUAGE

The official language of Iceland is Icelandic, which is considered a Germanic language. Icelanders like to think of their language as poetic and musical, and maintaining their language is an important part of Icelandic culture. Most Icelanders speak English and are happy to converse with tourists in English, but they are proud of their mother tongue and enjoy

Festivals

There's always something going on in Iceland—and whether it's the Viking Festival in June celebrating the country's roots, or the huge Iceland Airwaves music festival in the autumn, there's something for everyone.

February
Sónar Reykjavík: This three-day music festival in mid-February features local and international rock, pop, and electronic bands.

Reykjavík Food & Fun Festival (Reykjavík): During this three-day festival at the end of February, world-renowned chefs occupy kitchens at trendy Reykjavík restaurants, using fresh local ingredients and lots of imagination.

March
DesignMarch: Typically held in early March over four days, DesignMarch showcases the newest and best Icelandic design in pop up shops, lectures, and fun events around the city.

April
Reykjavík Blues Festival: For a week in early April, blues music enthusiasts from around the world descend on Reykjavík for this annual festival that features international musicians and local artists.

May
Reykjavík Arts Festival: For two weeks over late May/early June, Reykjavík is treated to exhibitions and outdoor installations of local and international artists.

June
Viking Festival: Just outside Reykjavík in Hafnarfjörður, the annual Viking

when foreign tourists give the language a go, even just a few words. The closest language to Icelandic is Faroese, which roughly 50,000 people speak, and the other close language spoken by a larger group is Norwegian. Many Icelanders can understand Norwegian, Swedish, and Danish due to some similarities. Learning Icelandic is a challenge for many foreigners because of the complex grammar and accent.

Alphabet
The Icelandic alphabet has 32 letters, including letters not known in the English language, such as Ð and Þ. The letter Ð represents the sound "th" as in "this," while Þ represents "th" as in "thin."

ICELANDIC NAMES
Iceland has a strident naming committee that must approve names parents wish to give their newborns, in the spirit of maintaining Icelandic culture. For that reason, you will find a lot of common first names, including Bjorn, Jón, Ólafur, Guðmundur, and Magnús for males, and Guðrun,

Festival in mid-June has fun reenactments of fights with traditional dress and weaponry, as well as food, music, and a market. The week-long festival is great for kids.

July
All Tomorrow's Parties: The major touring music festival found its way to Keflavík a few years ago. Local and international acts take the stage for three days in early July.

August
Reykjavík Jazz Festival: It may seem unexpected, but Icelanders have an affinity for jazz music, and they put on a great annual festival over five days in mid-August that features local and international musicians.

Reykjavík Culture Night: Held at the end of August, this day-long event is the biggest and most popular festival in Iceland, with more than 100,000 people participating. There's live music, food, and art to celebrate the end of the summer and Iceland's rich culture.

September
Reykjavík International Film Festival: Beginning at the end of September, this 11-day festival features short films, documentaries, and features from more than 40 countries.

October
Iceland Airwaves: The largest music festival of the year hits Iceland in late October/early November. More than 200 local and international artists perform at the five-day festival, which has attracted bands including Kraftwerk, Flaming Lips, and local band Of Monsters and Men.

Sara, and Anna for females. Very few Icelanders have surnames; instead, Iceland follows a patronymic system in which children are given their father's first name followed by -son or -dottir. If a man named Einar has a son named Johannes and a daughter named Anna, their names will be Johannes Einarsson and Anna Einarsdottir.

RELIGION
Icelanders have an interesting relationship with religion. Most of the country identifies as Lutheran (more than 70 percent), but most Icelanders aren't known to attend church regularly or be very vocal about their religious beliefs. While the majority of the country identifies as religious, Iceland is considered a liberal nation. There is no separation of church and state in Iceland; the National Church of Iceland is subsidized by Icelanders through a church tax. However, non-Lutherans can choose to have their church tax donated to designated charities.

Of Iceland's religious minorities, Catholics are the largest minority at about 4 percent, and there are about 1,000 Muslims estimated to call

Iceland home, as well as about 100 Jews. There is not a single synagogue in Iceland, as the Jewish population has not requested one, but a mosque was approved by Reykjavík in 2014, and construction is underway.

FOLKLORE

Icelanders have a spiritual connection to nature, which has been depicted through literature, paintings, and stories about the *huldufólk* or "hidden people." It's easy to understand why stories of *huldufólk* are prevalent once you experience the otherworldly nature of Iceland, including northern lights, crazy rock formations, howling wind, and desolate lava fields where it feels that anything can happen. Many of the hidden people stories originate in the lava fields, where unexplained phenomena, like broken farm equipment, could be explained away by saying "it must be the *huldufólk*." Indeed, Iceland's hidden people live among the rocks, and certain rocks are deemed "*huldufólk* churches." It's easy to dismiss the idea of hidden people, especially when the term is loosely translated as elves, but many Icelanders are not willing to deny the existence of hidden people. Does that mean that all Icelanders believe that elves physically walk among their human neighbors? Of course not. But it is part of their history and culture, and many Icelanders have a sense of humor about the foreign notion of *huldufólk*.

ARTS

Music

Music plays a large role in Icelandic society. There's still an emphasis on children learning to play instruments, and there are music schools around the country. It seems that everyone in Iceland is in at least one band. The earliest Icelandic music is called *rímur,* which is a sort of chanting style of singing that could include lyrics ranging from religious to descriptions of nature. Choirs are also very common in Iceland, and there are frequent performances in schools and churches that are usually well attended by the community.

As for modern music, Iceland boasts quite a few acts that have gained a following abroad. Of course, there's Björk, who put Iceland on the musical map back in the 1980s with her band, The Sugarcubes, and later her solo career. Icelanders tend to be quite proud of Björk, as an artist and an environmentalist. Sigur Rós became an indie favorite, and the band has been recording since 1994. Of Monsters and Men, Ólafur Arnalds, Amiina, Samaris, and GusGus are taking the world by storm. Reykjavík has cool venues to check out local bands and DJs and some great record shops to pick up the newest and latest Icelandic releases.

Literature

Iceland has a rich literary history. The sagas, considered the best-known specimens of Icelandic literature, are stories in prose describing events that took place in Iceland in the 10th and 11th centuries, during the so-called Saga Age. Focused on history, especially genealogical and family history, the sagas reflect the conflicts that arose within the societies of the second and third generations of Icelandic settlers. The authors of the sagas are unknown; *Egil's Saga* is believed to have been written by Snorri Sturluson, a 13th-century descendant of the saga's hero, but this remains uncertain. Widely read in school, the sagas are celebrated as an important part of Iceland's history.

Icelanders are voracious readers and love to write novels, prose, and poetry. The nation's most celebrated author is Halldór Laxness, who won a Nobel Prize for Literature in 1951 for his cherished novel *Independent People*. His tales have been translated into several languages and center on themes near and dear to Icelanders—nature, love, travel, and adventure. Other authors who have been translated into English (and other languages) include Sjón, Arnaldur Indriðason, and Einar Már Guðmundsson, among scores of others.

Crafts (Knitting)

Icelanders have been knitting for centuries, and it remains a common hobby today. Icelandic sheep have been the source of wool that's been keeping Icelanders warm for generations, and a traditional, modern sweater design emerged in the 1950s or so in the form of the *lopapeysa*. A *lopapeysa* has a distinctive yoke design around the neck opening, and they come in a variety of colors, with the most common colors being brown, gray, black, and off-white. Icelanders knit with *lopi* yarn, which contains both hairs and fleece of Icelandic sheep. The yarn is not spun, making it more difficult to work with than spun yarn, but the texture and insulation are unmistakable.

Essentials

Visas and Officialdom 99

Transportation 100

Accommodations and Food 101

Travel Tips 103

Information and Services 107

Visas and Officialdom

VISAS AND PASSPORTS

Visitors to Iceland must have a valid passport that will not expire within three months of your scheduled departure. Tourists from the United States, Canada, Australia, and New Zealand do not need a visa if they are traveling to Iceland for fewer than 90 days. If you want to stay longer, you need to apply for a residence permit at the Icelandic immigration office (www. utl.is). For Europeans, Iceland is part of the Schengen Agreement, which allows free travel between Iceland and European Economic Area (EEA) and European Union (EU) countries; visas are not necessary.

EMBASSIES

Icelandic Embassies

Iceland has embassies in a number of countries, including:

- **Canada:** 360 Albert St., Suite 710, Ottawa, ON K1R 7X7, tel. 613/482-1944, www.iceland.is/ca

- **United Kingdom:** 2A Hans St, London SW1X 0JE, tel. 20/7259-3999, www.iceland.is/uk

- **United States:** 2900 K St. NW, Suite 509, Washington, DC 20007, tel. 202/265-6653, www.iceland.is/us

Foreign Embassies in Iceland

If you have an emergency while traveling in Iceland and require assistance (for example, if you lose your passport), contact your embassy for help. Embassies in Reykjavík include:

- **Canada:** Túngata 14, tel. 354/575-6500, rkjvk@international.gc.ca

- **United Kingdom:** Laufásvegur 31, tel. 354/550-5100, info@britishembassy.is

- **United States:** Laufásvegur 21, tel. 354/595-2200, reykjavikconsular@state.gov

CUSTOMS

Getting through Customs in Iceland is quite easy when compared to most other countries in Europe.

Travelers can import duty-free alcoholic beverages and tobacco products as follows: 1 liter of spirits, 1 liter of wine, and 1 carton or 250g of other tobacco products; or 1 liter of spirits, 6 liters of beer, and 1 carton or 250g of other tobacco products; or 1.5 liters of wine, 6 liters of beer, and 1 carton or 250g of other tobacco products; or 3 liters wine and 1 carton or 250g of other tobacco products. The minimum age for bringing alcoholic beverages into Iceland is 20 years; for tobacco, it's 18 years.

Iceland has a zero-tolerance policy on drugs, and all meat, raw-egg products, and unpasteurized dairy will be confiscated.

For additional information, visit the official Customs website (www.tollur.is).

Transportation

GETTING THERE

Air

Keflavík International Airport (KEF, tel. 354/425-6000, www.kefairport.is), about 50 minutes west of Reykjavík, frequently gets kudos for being one of the best airports in Europe, and they're well deserved. Flying into Iceland is a pretty seamless experience. The country's main carrier, Icelandair (www.icelandair.com), serves more than 30 destinations in the United States, Canada, and Europe. Iceland's accessibility has been a main selling point as a travel destination because the country is just five hours from New York City and about three hours from London. Icelandair cleverly introduced an option years ago that allows North American travelers going on to Europe to stop over in Iceland for no extra cost. You can spend a couple days or longer to explore Iceland, and then continue on to your destination in Europe. The summer season is obviously the most expensive, with round-trip tickets that could exceed $1,000 from North America. Icelandair offers great deals during the winter months, when you can grab a round-trip ticket for around $500.

Sea

For those traveling from mainland Europe, a ferry can be a great option, especially if you want to bring a car, camper, or bicycle for the trip. Smyril Line (www.smyril-line.fo) is a Faroese company that runs the ferry *Norröna*, which goes to Iceland from Denmark, Norway, and the Faroe Islands. The ferry drops you off in Seyðisfjörður, in East Iceland, which is convenient for those traveling with cars and who want to spend time in the countryside. But, if you want to stay in the south, where Reykjavík and Golden Circle attractions are, a ferry may not be the best option. The timetable tends to change frequently, so check the website for the latest information.

ACCOMMODATIONS

Hotels

Iceland is not known for posh hotels offering every luxury that you desire. However, there is a good mix of "upscale" accommodations, mid-level boutiques, and budget hotels. The "fanciest" options on the island are in Reykjavík; namely 101 Hotel and Hótel Borg, which cater to guests who are willing to pay for top-notch service and amenities. Reykjavík also has midrange boutique or family-run options if you are looking for something a bit more formal than a guesthouse.

Outside of Reykjavík, hotels tend to be of the local chain-hotel ilk in the form of **Fosshotels** (www.fosshotel.is), **Hótel Edda** (www.hoteledda. is), and **Icelandair Hótels** (www.icelandairhotels.is). They are clean, comfortable, and reliable options.

When they compare hotel prices to those in other European countries, some tourists feel that they don't get their money's worth. In fairness, Iceland is a more popular destination than it was 20 years ago, but it's still not meant to be a budget destination. In short, accommodations do cost a lot. Be prepared for slightly shocking rates, especially in the summer months.

Guesthouses

The most prevalent form of accommodations on the island is the guesthouse set-up. Guesthouses range from comfortable bed-and-breakfasts that offer shared bathrooms and cooking facilities to more design-conscious options that are chic, modern, and fun. Some guesthouses in Reykjavík can still have "hotel-like" prices, as the competition for scoring a room in the high season has become almost a contact sport. Outside Reykjavík, however, guesthouses could be a good way to save a little money, depending on where you book. Always book a room in advance, as it's not recommended to leave where you will lay your head to chance.

Hostels

Hostels are another great option for the budget traveler, but as in guesthouses, beds tend to fill up, so make sure you book far in advance, especially in the summer. Some hostels in Reykjavík, like Kex Hostel and Loft Hostel, cater to young, music-conscious travelers, and beds are almost an afterthought. There is frequently live music in the lounge areas, and the bar is always packed with locals and tourists. Other hostel options cater to a more mature crowd looking to avoid the expensive hotel rates. Hlemmur Square would be a good option for those travelers. Outside of Reykjavík, hostels are prevalent and it's key to book ahead.

Sleeping Bag Accommodations

Some guesthouses and hostels around Iceland offer travelers sleeping bag accommodations, which can be great for the budget traveler. For a low price, guests are allowed to sleep in their sleeping bags and have access to shared bathroom facilities.

FOOD
Typical Fare

The description of Icelandic food that you get depends on whom you ask, although it can't be disputed that fish and lamb take center stage. Typical fare can range from light to hearty. Local produce means what can survive outdoors (potatoes, rhubarb, moss) and what is grown in greenhouses (tomatoes, cucumbers, broccoli, etc.). Most of Iceland's food is imported, and it isn't cheap.

Local fish includes cod (fresh/salted), salmon, lobster, mussels, halibut, trout, and haddock. A classic Icelandic dish is whitefish cooked in a white sauce with potatoes and onions. A popular snack is hardfish, which is like a whitefish jerky, where the fish is dried and seasoned.

As for meat, lamb is the most prevalent, but there is plenty of beef, pork, and chicken in the Icelandic diet. Some Icelanders also indulge in horse and whale meat as well.

Hot dogs are wildly popular among Icelanders. Called *pylsur,* Icelandic hot dogs are done up in a traditional bun with chopped onions, mustard, ketchup, crispy fried onions, and pickled mayonnaise. They're delicious.

Dairy is an important part of Icelanders' diets, including milk, cheese, butter, and the yogurt-like soft cheese called *skyr,* which you should try. It's very tasty and chock-full of protein. Icelanders are also known to eat ice cream all year long, despite the weather. There are quite a few popular ice cream shops around Reykjavík, and the ice cream sections in supermarkets offer an astounding number of locally produced choices.

ESSENTIALS
ACCOMMODATIONS AND FOOD

Þingvellir National Park

Once a year, Icelanders celebrate the traditional foods of the nation, which sustained their ancestors through the ages. The winter festival, called Þorrablót, features *svið* (singed lamb head), blood pudding, lamb intestines and stomach, ram's testicles, fermented shark, seal flippers, hardfish, and rye bread. The food that gets the most attention from foreigners is rotten shark or *hákarl,* which is meat from Greenland shark. The flesh is put through an interesting process, where it is buried for at least two months and then is hung for another three or four months to cure. If you dare, *hákarl* is available in small containers for sale. It is an experience you will not forget—if not the taste, then definitely the smell.

Finding a Restaurant

Reykjavík is home to some excellent fine dining establishments and casual eateries, but eating cheaply in Reykjavík, or on the island as a whole, is not easy. Hours tend to change depending on the season, but for the most part restaurants open their doors for lunch around 11:30am, and kitchens tend to close around 10pm.

Outside of Reykjavík, you will find a lot of fish and lamb restaurants that focus on local cuisine, but inside the two main cities, you have a lot to choose from. You will find sushi, tapas, Indian, hamburger joints, noodle bars, kebab houses, and Italian restaurants to name a few. International cuisine has been growing in popularity over the last 20 years, and new and interesting spots are always cropping up.

Drinking

The water in Iceland is pure and some of the tastiest in the world. Drinking from the tap is common and safe, and bottled water is frowned upon. Iceland is also a coffee-drinking nation. If you're a tea drinker, you will find some basic choices in coffee shops, but Icelanders are crazy about their coffee.

As for alcohol, Icelanders do have a reputation for indulging, but given the expensive prices, beer is the drink of choice when going out to a bar. And, believe it or not, beer is still relatively new to Iceland. A countrywide alcohol ban went into effect in 1915; the ban was relaxed in phases, with first wine and then strong liquors permitted, and beer eventually became legal to sell in 1989. Outside of bars, alcohol is available only at the government-run shops called Vínbúðin.

Travel Tips

WOMEN TRAVELERS

Iceland is regularly ranked as being one of the best countries in the world in which to be a woman and a mother. Icelanders are proud to have elected the first woman president in the world as well as the first openly gay prime minister (a woman). However, Iceland is not a utopia. Women are subject to incidents of theft, intimidation, and physical violence. Always keep your wits about you, and if you are a victim of crime, contact the police at the emergency number 112.

GAY AND LESBIAN TRAVELERS

Iceland is a leader in equality, and Reykjavík is one of the most gay-friendly cities in Europe. What many travelers find refreshing is that there is not just tolerance for gay, lesbian, bisexual, and transgendered individuals, but overwhelming love and acceptance of their fellow Icelanders. For instance, the gay pride festival, Reykjavík Pride, which takes place every August, attracts approximately 100,000 participants, for a country of just 320,000 people. Think about that. As for laws, the LGBT community is protected from discrimination, gay marriage was legalized in 2010, and hate crimes are few and far between. For such a small population, it's hard to say there's a "gay scene," but there is one gay bar in Reykjavík, Kiki Queer Bar. More information can be found at the Pink Iceland website (www. pinkiceland.is).

TRAVELING WITH CHILDREN

Children are the center of Icelandic society, and tourists traveling with children will feel right at home, whether in restaurants, museums, or child-appropriate tours. The island is a safe place for children, and many foreign travelers raise an eyebrow at how carefree parents can appear—whether it's a child walking around a shop, or an unaccompanied pram outside a coffeehouse. It's not irresponsible parenting, just a reflection on how safe a society Iceland is. While Iceland is safe, it needs to be said to always take care to watch out for the elements, whether it's high winds, a slippery surface, or cracks in a walking path.

As for attractions and restaurants, there are frequently child rates for museums, tours, and children's options on menus. Discounts can be a great as 50 percent off for children under the age of 16.

TRAVELERS WITH DISABILITIES

Iceland has taken great strides in making as many tourist-related sites as wheelchair-friendly as possible. Visitors in wheelchairs will find that most museums, swimming pools, and restaurants provide access, as do transportation services. For instance, Keflavík International Airport and all domestic airlines can accommodate travelers in wheelchairs, and many buses come with automatic ramps to allow for easy boarding.

For more information on accessible travel, get in touch with the organization Þekkingarmiðstöð Sjálfsbjargar (tel. 354/550-0118, www. thekkingarmidstod.is). While the website is almost entirely in Icelandic only, information on traveling in Iceland has been translated into English (www.thekkingarmidstod.is/adgengi/accessible-tourism-in-iceland), and employees are happy to assist in English.

For information on services available to deaf travelers, contact the **Icelandic Association of the Deaf** (www.deaf.is), and for services for the sight-impaired, contact the **Icelandic Association of the Blind** (www.blind.is).

WHAT TO PACK
Clothing

The key to dressing warm and being comfortable in Iceland is layers. Depending on the weather, it can be cotton T-shirt, fleece or sweater, parka or windbreaker, and perhaps a hat, scarf, and gloves. If it's summer and the sun is shining, it's common to see locals wearing a T-shirt in 15°C (60°F) weather. It's important to keep comfortable and add layers if the temperature warrants it. If you're out hiking, wearing waterproof gear along with proper hiking attire is key. Make sure fabrics are breathable and comfortable and under layers are cotton. Formal attire in Iceland is reserved for work or funerals, but if you want to bring a nice outfit along for a "fancy" dinner, by all means, pack something, but you won't find stringent dress codes anywhere on this island. Lastly, a bathing suit is necessary. Even if you think you won't take a dip in a pool or hot spring, the temptation might be too great. Pack at least one.

Outerwear

Because the temperature varies so much depending on time of day, season, and where you are in the country, it's a good idea to bring a hat, scarf, and gloves. As for jackets, the best advice is to bring something waterproof; whether it's a windbreaker for summer or a parka for winter, you are likely to encounter rain at some point on your trip. If you need to go shopping for warmer layers in Iceland, expect to pay. Clothes are not cheap in Iceland.

Footwear

Again, if you are staying in Reykjavík for the duration of your trip, and

Reykjavík Pride festival

don't plan to climb mountains, you don't need to invest in an expensive pair of hiking boots. That said, if you do plan to be outdoors quite a bit, hiking boots are a great idea. You will need a pair of shoes that can withstand rain, rocks, ice, mud, puddles, sand, and sometimes snow. It's recommended to buy boots in your home country because shoes can be expensive in Iceland, and it's not the best idea to break in a brand-new pair of boots if you plan to do a lot of walking and/or climbing. Comfort is key. Socks are also important to consider. You want socks that are breathable yet thick enough to keep you comfortable in your shoes/boots.

HEALTH AND SAFETY
Medical Services
The Icelandic health-care system is top-notch, with hospitals in each large town and health clinics in smaller villages and hamlets. Most doctors, nurses, and emergency medical staff speak English, and non-EU citizens must pay for health services provided. If you are having a medical emergency, dial the number 112. Pharmacies (called *apótek*) hold everything from prescription medication to aspirin. Some tourists from North America find it frustrating that cold medicine and aspirin cannot be bought in supermarkets, just at the pharmacy. Pharmacies are typically open 10am-9pm Monday-Friday, 10am-4pm Saturday, and closed on Sunday and public holidays.

Weather
Weather is the number one safety concern in Iceland, trumping everything from violent crime to volcanic eruptions. The main danger is how fast weather can change. It could be a bright, sunny day when you head out on a trek in the highlands, but there could be a storm brewing that will bring high winds, rain, hail, and snow. And the storm could pass as quickly as it arrived. The joke among locals is that if you don't like the weather in Iceland, wait five minutes. The best defense against inclement weather is to closely monitor weather forecasts and obey advisories. You can check frequently updated forecasts at www.vedur.is. Icelanders deal with the weather by being flexible and never confirming plans far in advance. They learn to adapt after a lifetime of battling gale force winds.

Temperatures in Iceland can vary, but on average Reykjavík's winter season is warmer than New York City's. That said, always dress for the environment and the activity you are about to embark on. If you are staying within Reykjavík's city limits, dress comfortably with layers and waterproof gear. If you're out in the evening, have a hat, scarf, gloves, and warm gear at the ready.

Crime
Crime is quite low in Iceland and is mostly limited to theft and vandalism; violent crime is rare. Be vigilant in protecting your possessions (especially bicycles) and trust your instincts. If you're out at night on Laugavegur in

downtown Reykjavík on weekends, you might encounter loud and drunk locals or tourists. Don't engage with drunken people; continue about your business. If you are a victim of a crime, contact the police by dialing the emergency number, 112; all police officers are proficient in English.

Information and Services

TOURIST INFORMATION

Visit Iceland (www.visiticeland.com) is the main tourist information website for the country. The website has information on accommodations and activities for each region in Iceland.

MONEY

Iceland is not a cheap place to visit. Don't be fooled by the news stories that declared Iceland cut prices to accommodate tourists after its economic crisis of 2008. That period was brief, and Iceland remains an expensive destination. Prices on accommodations, food, gas, and everyday necessities remain high. Here is a list showing prices of common items.

- Milk (1 L): 131ISK
- Loaf of bread: 232ISK
- Dozen eggs: 514ISK
- Apples (1 kg): 388ISK
- Potatoes (1 kg): 223ISK
- Coke/Pepsi: 265ISK
- Meal for two: 10,500ISK
- Domestic beer: 900ISK
- Bottle of wine: 2,100ISK
- Pack of cigarettes: 1,200ISK
- Bus ticket (one way): 350ISK
- Gasoline (1 L): 250ISK

Currency

The official currency of Iceland is the króna (abbreviated kr or ISK). The króna fluctuates often; at the time of writing, the exchange rate was 125ISK to US$1.

There are banknotes in the amount of 500, 1,000, 5,000, and 10,000 and coins in the amount of 1, 5, 10, 50, and 100 kronur. Coins are handy for having exact change for the bus. Cash overall is not a popular payment method; locals are known to use debit and credit cards for just about every transaction.

Currency exchange is available at the airport and banks as well as tourist information offices. Your best bet to get the best exchange is to use your credit card. ATMs are available at all banks as well as supermarkets and other shops.

Banks

Banking hours are 9:15am-4pm Monday-Friday, and ATMs are available 24/7. There may be a limit on the amount of cash you can withdraw per your home bank's policy.

Tax-Free Shopping

As tourists encounter high prices for everything from accommodations to food, it only seems fair that you get a break when it comes to shopping.

A refund of local Value-Added Tax (VAT) is available to all visitors in Iceland. The refund will result in a reduction of up to 15 percent of the retail price, provided departure from Iceland is within three months after the date of purchase.

The fine print is that the refund does not apply to food or accommodations and the purchase must exceed 4,000ISK (VAT included) per store. Shops will provide you with a tax-free form (ask the store clerk for a "tax-free check"). Make sure you tuck the forms all away and redeem the rebate at the cash-refund office at Keflavík Airport before your flight. There, you will get an immediate cash refund.

You can also submit the receipts and paperwork by mail for a rebate on your credit card. This, of course, can take considerably longer.

Tipping

Tipping is very new to Iceland. Workers in bars, restaurants, and hotels, as well as taxi drivers, earn a living wage and are not dependent on tips. In recent years, tip jars have cropped up in coffeehouses and bars, but it's just tourists who tend to tip.

MAPS

To properly navigate Iceland, you need maps. That's a given. Lucky for you, they are available all over the island. You can pick up all-inclusive maps for the entire island as well as regional maps, road maps, and hiking maps at tourist information centers, bookstores, and gas stations. If you have the chance to purchase maps before your trip, do so, as they will likely be a lot cheaper in your home country. However, if you plan to stay in Reykjavík for the duration of your trip, it's not necessary to buy a map because quite a few free maps do a nice job detailing downtown Reykjavík.

COMMUNICATIONS AND MEDIA
Telephone

The country code for Iceland is 354. There are no area codes; if you are calling from within the country, just dial the seven-digit phone number and you will connect.

Icelanders love their mobile phones, and for that reason pay phones

Holidays in Iceland

Businesses in Iceland close on the following holidays:

- January 1: **New Year's Day**

- March or April: **Maundy Thursday**

- March or April: **Good Friday**

- March or April: **Easter Sunday**

- March or April: **Easter Monday**

- First Thursday after April 18: **First day of summer**

- May 1: **Labor Day**

- May or June: **Ascension Day**

- May or June: **Whitsun**

- May or June: **Whit Monday**

- June 17: **Icelandic National Day** (commemorates achieving independence from Denmark in 1944)

- First Monday in August: **Trading Day**

- December 24: **Christmas Eve**

- December 25: **Christmas Day**

- December 26: **Second day of Christmas**

- December 31: **New Year's Eve**

became obsolete several years ago. You can purchase international phone cards at local shops (called *sjoppas*) as well as the post office and gas stations. SIM cards are also available from providers **Vodafone** (www.vodafone.is) and **Siminn** (www.siminn.is) and can be purchased from phone retail shops, gas stations, and the airport.

Cell phone coverage in the countryside is surprisingly strong.

Internet Access
Iceland is wired, with Wi-Fi hot spots all over the country. Hotels typically have free Wi-Fi as do many coffeehouses.

Media
Given its small population, it's refreshing to see Iceland as such a

die-hard newspaper town. Locals have several Icelandic-language print publications and websites to choose from, but publishers haven't forgotten about English-language readers. The *Reykjavík Grapevine* (www.grapevine.is) is the unofficial guide to music, museum exhibitions, restaurant reviews, and just about every cultural event in the city. The website is updated daily, and the free print edition comes out biweekly in the summer and monthly in the winter. *Iceland Review* (www.icelandreview.com) is the main English-language glossy magazine on the island. You will find in-depth features on travel, culture, and business issues as well as gorgeous photography.

RUV (www.ruv.is) is Iceland's national public-service broadcasting organization, which consists of one television channel and two radio stations. RUV's television programs include news, dramas, documentaries, as well as programming from foreign countries, including the United States, Denmark, and Sweden.

TIME ZONE

Iceland uses Greenwich mean time (GMT). However, the country does not observe daylight saving time, so Iceland is either four or five hours ahead of New York time, depending on the time of year.

As for the amount of daylight, what you've heard is true. The summers are full of long days, and darkness reigns supreme in the winter. To give you an idea of what that means, here are daylight hours for Reykjavík at different times of year:

• January 1: sunrise 11:20am, sunset 3:45pm

• April 1: sunrise 6:45am, sunset 8:20pm

• July 1: sunrise 3:05am, sunset midnight

• October 1: sunrise 7:30am, sunset 7pm

WEIGHTS AND MEASURES

Iceland uses the metric system. With regard to electricity, the standard voltage is 230 V and the standard frequency is 50 Hz. The power sockets that are used are type F, for plugs with two round pins. If you forget to bring an adapter, they can be purchased in most bookstores and tourist shops.

Resources

Glossary

austur: east
bíó: movie theater
bær: farm
bíll: car
bjarg: rock, cliff
dalur: valley
ey: island
fjall: mountain
fjörður: fjord
fljót: river
flugvöllur: airport
foss: waterfall
gata: street
geysir: erupting hot spring
herbergi: room
hestur: horse
hraun: lava field
hradbanki: ATM
huldufólk: hidden people
höfn: harbor
Ísland: Iceland
jökull: glacier
kirkja: church
kort: map
laug: swimming pool
lopapeysa: Icelandic knitted sweater
lundi: puffin
norður: north
safn: museum
sími: telephone
stræti: street
strætó: bus
suður: south
sumar: summer

tjörn: pond
torg: town square
vatn: water
vestur: west
vetur: winter
veður: weather

Icelandic Phrasebook

Icelandic is not the easiest language to understand. It's a North Germanic language that is related to Norwegian, Danish, and Swedish, but it has the added difficulty of declensions that the other languages lack. Icelandic nouns are declined in four cases, which stumps many people. Fortunately, just about everyone in Iceland speaks English.

PRONUNCIATION

Pronunciation can be very tricky, but Icelanders are thrilled when tourists give their language a shot. Be warned, though; if you attempt to speak an Icelandic phrase, your accent will tell them you're a foreigner, and they most likely will answer you in English.

Vowels

Some vowels in Icelandic have accent marks that modify the sound of each vowel. Vowels can come in long or short forms. In Icelandic, all vowels can be long or short. Vowels are long when they are in single-syllable words or when they form the penultimate syllable in two-syllable words.

A a like the "a" in "land"
Á á like "ow" in "cow"
E e like the "e" in "set"
É é like "ye" in "yet"
I i like "i" in "sit"
Í í like "ee" in "feet"
O o like the "o" in "not"
Ó ó like the "o" in "flow"
U u like the "u" in "put"
Ú ú like the "oo" in "soon"
Y y like the "i" in "sit"
Ý ý like the "ee" in "feet"
Æ æ like the "i" in "file"
Ö ö like the "ur" in "lure"

Consonants

Ð ð like "th" in "this"
J j like "y" in "year"

R r rolled, like Spanish "r"

Þ þ like "th" in "thin"

BASIC AND COURTEOUS EXPRESSIONS

Hello *Halló*

Good morning *Góðan dag*

Good evening *Gott kvold*

How are you? *Hvað segir þu?*

Very well, thank you *Mjog gott, takk fyrir*

Good *Allt gott*

Not OK, bad *Ekki okei*

So-so *Bara fint*

OK *Allt í lagí*

And you? *En þu?*

Thank you *Takk fyrir*

Goodbye *Bless*

Nice to see you *Gaman að sjo þig*

See you later *Sjamust*

Please *Takk*

Yes *Ja*

No *Nei*

I don't know. *Ég skil ekki.*

Just a moment. *Augnablik.*

Excuse me. *Afsakið.*

What is your name? *Hvað heiti þu?*

Do you speak English? *Talarðu ensku?*

I don't speak Icelandic well. *Ég tala ekki íslensku svo vel.*

I don't understand. *Ég skil ekki.*

How do you say ... in Icelandic? *Hvernig segir maður ... á íslensku?*

My name is ... . *Ég heiti ... .*

What's your name? *Hvað heitir þú?*

TERMS OF ADDRESS

I *ég*

you *þu*

he/him *hann*

she/her *hun*

we *við*

they *þeir*

girl *stelpa*

boy *strakur*

man *maður*

woman *kona*

wife *eiginkona*

husband *eiginmaður*

friend *vinur*

son *sonur*

daughter *dottir*

brother *bróðir*

sister *systir*

father *pabbi*

mother *mamma*

grandfather *afi*

grandmother *amma*

ACCOMMODATIONS

hotel *hótel*

guesthouse *gistiheimilið, gistihúsið*

Is there a room? *Áttu laus herbergi?*

May I see the room first? *Má ég sjá herbergið fyrst?*

What is the rate? *Hvað kostar það?*

Is there something cheaper? *Ódýrara herbergi?*

single room *einsmanns herbergi*

double room *tveggjamanna herbergi*

bathroom *klósetti*

shower *sturtu*

towels *handklæði*

soap *sapa*

toilet paper *salernispappír*

sheets *rúmfötum*

key *lykill*

heater *hitari*

manager *framkvæmdastjóri*

FOOD

I'm hungry. *Ég er svangur.*

menu *matseðil*

May I have …? *Get ég fengið …?*

glass *glas*

fork *gaffall*

knife *hnifur*

spoon *skeið*

breakfast *morgunmatur*

lunch *hádegisverður*

dinner *kvöldmatur*

the check *reikninginn*

soda *gos*

coffee *kaffi*

tea *te*

water *vatn*

beer *bjór*
wine *vín*
white wine *hvítvín*
red wine *rauðvín*
milk *mjólk*
juice *safi*
cream *rjómi*
sugar *sykur*
eggs *eggjum*
cheese *osti*
yogurt *jógúrt*
almonds *möndlu*
cake *kaka*
bread *brauð*
butter *smjör*
salt *salt*
pepper *pipar*
garlic *hvítlaukur*
salad *salat*
vegetables *grænmeti*
carrot *gulrót*
corn *korn*
cucumber *agúrka*
lettuce *kál*
mushroom *sveppir*
onion *laukur*
potato *kartöflu*
spinach *spinat*
tomato *tómatar*
fruit *ávöxtum*
apple *epli*
orange *appelsína*
fish *fiski*
meat *kjöti*
lamb *lamb*
beef *nautakjöti*
chicken *kjúklingi*
pork *svínakjöt*
bacon *beikon*
ham *skinka*

SHOPPING

money *peningar*
What is the exchange rate? *Hvað er gengið á?*
Do you accept credit cards? *Tekur þú greiðslukort?*

How much does it cost? *Hvað kostar það?*

expensive *dýr*

cheap *ódýr*

more *meira*

less *minna*

a little *smá*

too much *of mikið*

HEALTH

Help me! *Hjálp!*

I am ill. *Ég er veikur.*

I need a doctor. *Ég þarf lækni.*

hospital *sjúkrahús*

pharmacy *apótek*

pain *verkir*

fever *hiti*

headache *höfuðverkur*

stomachache *magaverki*

burn *brunablettur*

cramp *krampa*

nausea *ógleði*

vomiting *uppköst*

antibiotic *sýklalyf*

pill *pilla*

aspirin *aspirín*

ointment *smyrsli*

cotton *bómull*

condoms *smokkur*

toothbrush *tannbursta*

toothpaste *tannkrem*

dentist *tannlæknir*

TRANSPORTATION

Where is the ...? *Hvar er ...?*

How do I get to ...? *Hvernig kemst ég til ...?*

the bus station *strætóstöðin*

the bus stop *strætóstopp*

Where is the bus going? *Hvert fer þessi strætó/rúta?*

taxi *taxi*

boat *bátur*

airport *flugvöllur*

A one-way ticket to ... *Einn miða, aðra leiðina til ...*

A round-trip ticket to ... *Einn miða, báðar leiðir til ...*

Stop here. *Hætta hér.*

I want to rent a car. *Get ég leigt bil.*

entrance *inngangur*
exit *útgangur*
to the; toward the *til*
right *hægri*
left *vinstri*
straight ahead *beint áfram*
past the … *framhjá …*
before the … *á undan …*
opposite the … *á móti …*
Watch for the … *Leita að …*
intersection *gatnamót*
street *stræti*
north; south *norður; suður*
east; west *austur; vestur*

STREET SIGNS

Stop *Stans*
One Way *Einstefna*
Yield *Biðskylda*
No Parking *Engin Bílastæði*
Speed Limit *Hámarkshraði*

AT THE GAS STATION

gas station *bensínstöð*
gasoline (petrol) *bensín*
diesel *disel*
garage *verkstæði*
air *loft*
water *vatn*
oil change *olíu breyting*
tow truck *draga vörubíl*

VERBS

to buy *að kaupa*
to eat *að borða*
to climb *að klifra*
to do or make *að gera*
to go *að fara*
to love *að elska*
to want *að vilja*
to need *að þurfa*
to read *að lesa*
to write *að skrifa*
to stop *að hætta*
to arrive *til koma*

to stay *að vera*
to leave *að fara*
to look for *að leita*
to give *að gefa*
to carry *að bera*
to have *að hafa*

NUMBERS

zero *null*
one *einn*
two *tveir*
three *prir*
four *fjorir*
five *fimm*
six *sex*
seven *sjo*
eight *atta*
nine *niu*
10 *tiu*
11 *ellefu*
12 *tólf*
13 *þrettán*
14 *fjórtán*
15 *fimmtán*
16 *sextán*
17 *sautján*
18 *átján*
19 *nítján*
20 *tuttugu*
21 *tuttugu og einn*
30 *prjatiu*
40 *fjorutiu*
50 *fimmtiu*
60 *sextiu*
70 *sjotiu*
80 *attatiu*
90 *niutiu*
100 *hundrað*
101 *hundrað og einn*
200 *tvö hundruð*
500 *fimm hundrað*
1,000 *þúsund*
100,000 *hundrað þúsund*
1,000,000 *milljón*

TIME

What time is it? *Hvað er klukkan?*
It's one o'clock. *Klukkan er eitt.*
morning *morgunn*
afternoon *eftir hádegi*
evening *kvöld*
night *nótt*
midnight *miðnætti*

DAYS AND MONTHS

Monday *mánudagur*
Tuesday *þriðjudagur*
Wednesday *miðvikudagur*
Thursday *fimmtudagur*
Friday *föstudagur*
Saturday *laugardagur*
Sunday *sunnudagur*
day *dagur*
today *í dag*
tomorrow *á morgun*
yesterday *í gær*
January *janúar*
February *febrúar*
March *mars*
April *april*
May *mai*
June *juni*
July *juli*
August *ágúst*
September *september*
October *október*
November *nóvember*
December *desember*
early *snemma*
late *seint*
later *seinna*
before *áður en*

Suggested Reading

Guðmundsson, Einar Már. *Angels of the Universe*. 1997. This is a startling tale of a young man struggling with mental illness, set in Iceland in the 1960s. The protagonist, Paul, retreats into his own fantasy world, while friends and family come along for the ride. The book is disturbing at times, funny at others, and almost impossible to put down. It was made into a film in 2000, which was wildly popular in Iceland.

Helgason, Hallgrímur. *101 Reykjavik*. 2007. The protagonist, Hlynur, is a lazy, unemployed twentysomething who lives with his mother, watches a lot of pornography, and hangs out in bars in downtown Reykjavík. His life takes a turn when a former girlfriend announces she is pregnant and Hlynur becomes obsessed with his mother's lesbian lover. It's a fun, unexpected tale that was made into a popular movie in Iceland.

Indriðason, Arnaldur. *Jar City*. 2006. Arnaldur is Iceland's leading mystery author. He pens about one book a year, which is great since his tales are so addicting. *Jar City* was the first of Arnaldur's books to feature detective Erlendur Sveinsson, who is a complicated man with a troubled relationship with his family and an obsession with solving Reykjavík's violent crimes. Other characters include his partner, Sigurður Óli, and a female colleague, Elínborg.

Kellogg, Robert. *The Sagas of Icelanders*. 2001. This huge volume includes 10 sagas and 7 shorter tales that give a wonderful overview of Iceland's history and literature. If you're looking for a short introduction, this isn't it. It's comprehensive and glorious.

Laxness, Halldór. *Independent People*. 1946. Laxness remains Iceland's sole recipient of the Nobel Prize for Literature for his novel *Independent People*. The tale follows the life of a Bjartur, a sheep farmer, as he grapples with life, loss, and the sacrifices he made to achieve independence. If you're going to read one Icelandic novel, this should be it.

Internet Resources

Icelandic Tourist Board
www.visiticeland.com
Iceland's tourist board provides a website with pages and pages of information for travelers. The site offers information on festivals, shopping, national parks, and outdoor activities like hiking, birdwatching, whale-watching, and catching the northern lights in the wintertime. There's also information on accommodations, tour operators, and maps.

www.icelandreview.com

Iceland's main English-language magazine provides features on everything from culture to travel to politics. The website underwent a revamp in 2014 and is worth checking out for in-depth articles as well as columns written by locals.

Reykjavík Grapevine

www.grapevine.is

Reykjavík's go-to English language newspaper, which is published biweekly in the summer and monthly in the winter, also maintains a website. You can bone up on local news as well as check out a listings section that details concerts, art exhibitions, and bars.

Visit South Iceland

www.south.is

Covering the south as well as the Reykjanes Peninsula, this tourism site offers detailed information on driving routes, maps, accommodations options, and tour operators. This region encompasses the Blue Lagoon.

A

accessibility: 104-105
accommodations: 39-53, 101-102, 114;
    see also specific place
air quality: 87-88
air travel: 54, 100
Álafoss Wool Factory Shop: 57
alcohol: 103
All Tomorrow's Parties: 68, 95
Almannagjá: 76
alphabet: 94, 112-113
Alþing: 20, 76, 77, 80, 89, 91
Alþingishúsið (Parliament House): 20
apartments: 43-44
Arnarson, Ingólfur: 9, 18, 89
Árnason, Jón Gunnar: 21-22
arts and crafts: 96-97; see also
    shopping
Ásmundarsafn: 14
Ásmundur Sveinsson: 14
Aurora Reykjavík: 22

B

banks/banking: 92, 108
Bar 11: 7, 28
Bárðarbunga volcano: 87
bars: 27-28
beer: 103
beverages: 103
biking: see cycling
birds/bird-watching: 6, 25, 66, 70, 71
Bláa Lónið (Blue Lagoon): 7, 10, 37, 71-
    72, 73, 74, 88
Blue Lagoon (Bláa Lónið): 7, 10, 37, 71-
    72, 73, 74, 88
books/bookstores: 33-34, 119-120
Borgartún (Höfði House): 21
Buddha Café: 6, 44-45
bus travel: 54, 55; see also specific place
Byggðasafn Garðskaga (Folk Museum):
    70

C

Café Babalu: 6, 51
Café Haiti: 6, 51
camping: 70, 73, 82
cell phones: 108-109
children, tips for traveling with: 104-
    105
Christianity: 89, 95-96
Church of Hallgrímur: see
    Hallgrímskirkja

climate: 86, 106
clothing: 35-36, 105
coffeehouses: 51-52, 108, 109
costs: 107
crafts: 97; see also shopping
crime: 106-107
cultural customs: 93-97
Culture House (Þjóðmenningarhúsið): 16
currency: 93, 107-108
customs, cultural: 93-97
customs regulations: 99-100
cycling: 24, 56, 72-73

D

dance clubs: 26-27
demographics: 93
DesignMarch: 30, 94
disabilities, tips for travelers with:
    104-105
diving: 78
doctors: 106
driving: 55

E

earthquakes: 87
economy: 92-93
Einar Jónsson: 17
Einar Jónsson Museum: 17
Eldey Island: 71
electrical current: 110
Elíasson, Ólafur: 20
embassies: 99
emergency services: 54
energy: 92-93
entertainment/events: 26-31
ethnicity: 93
European Union: 90-91
EVE Fanfest: 30
events: 30-31, 63, 68, 94-95, 109
Eyjafjallajökull volcano: 87

F

ferries: 65, 100
festivals/events: 30-31, 63, 68, 94-95, 109
Fishermen Memorial: 72
fish/fishing: 24, 79, 92
Fiskfelagid: 6, 48
fissure vents: 87
Fjölskyldu- og Húsdýragarðinum
    (Reykjavík Zoo): 22-23
Fjörukráin (Viking Village): 63
folklore: 96

Folk Museum (Byggðasafn Garðskaga): 70
food: 46-54, 102-103, 114-115; *see also specific place*
footwear: 105-106

G

Galleri Laugarvatn: 80
Garður: 69-70
gay/lesbian travelers, tips for: 28, 30, 104
geography: 86
geology: 87
geothermal energy: 92-93
Gerðarsafn (Kópavogur Art Museum): 60-61
Gerður Helgadóttir: 60-61
geysers: 81-82
Geysir: 81-83
glaciers: 88
Gljúfrasteinn: 57
glossary: 111-112
Golden Circle: 76-84; map 77
Golden Falls (Gullfoss): 83-84
golf: 73
government: 91-92
Grasagardur Reykjavíkur (Reykjavík Botanical Garden): 23
gratuities: 108
Grímsson, Ólafur Ragnar: 91
Grindavík: 71-75
Grindavík Swimming Pool: 73
guesthouses: 42-43, 101; *see also accommodations*
Gullfoss (Golden Falls): 83-84
Gunnlaugsson, Sigmundur Davíð: 91

H

Hafnarborg Center of Culture and Fine Art: 63
Hafnarfjörður: 62-64
Hafnarfjörður Museum: 62-63
Hafnarhús: 11-14
Hafstein, Hannes: 90
hákarl meat: 103
Hallgrímskirkja: 6, 10, 16-17
Hallgrímur Pétursson: 16
handicrafts: *see crafts*
Handprjónasamband Íslands (Handknitting Association of Iceland): 6, 36
Hannes Hafstein: 90
Harpa concert hall: 7, 10, 20-21
health: 106-107, 116
Hekla volcano: 87
Helgadóttir, Gerður: 60-61
Hið Íslenzka Reðasafn (Icelandic Phallological Museum): 17

hiking: 10, 57-59, 66, 75, 79, 105-106
history: 89-91
Hlemmur bus station: 55
Höfði House (Borgartún): 21
holidays: 109
Holuhraun: 87
horses/horseback riding: 59, 63, 66, 79
hospitals: 54, 106
hostels: 42-43, 101; *see also specific place*
hot dogs: 50, 102
hotels: 39-42, 101; *see also accommodations*
hot springs: 71-72, 80, 88
Hrím: 6, 32
huldufólk: 96
Húrra: 6, 26, 28
Húsatóftir Golf Course: 73

IJ

ice cream: 52-53, 102
Iceland Airwaves: 31, 34, 95
Icelandic language: 93-94, 111-119
Icelandic Opera (Íslenska Óperan): 29
Icelandic Phallological Museum (Hið Íslenzka Reðasafn): 17
Icelandic Sagas: 96-97, 120
Icelandic Symphony Orchestra (Sinfóníuhljómsveit Íslands): 29
Iceland Review: 110, 120
Imagine Peace Tower: 65
independence: 90
information/services: 53-54, 107-110, 120; *see also specific place*
Ingólfur Arnarson: 9, 18, 89
Internet access: 109
Internet resources: 120-121
Íslenska Óperan (Icelandic Opera): 29
Jón Gunnar Árnason: 21-22
Jónsson, Einar: 17

K

Katla volcano: 87
Keflavík: 66-69
Keflavík base: 66, 90, 91-92
Keflavík International Airport: 54, 69, 100, 104
Kex Hostel: 6, 29, 43, 101
Kjarval, Jóhannes: 14
Kjarvalsstaðir: 14
knitting: 57, 97
Kol & Salt: 6, 18
Kópavogur: 60-62
Kópavogur Art Museum (Gerðarsafn): 60-61
Kópavogur Swimming Pool: 61
Kringlan: 38

króna: 107-108
Krýsuvík geothermal area: 75

L

language: 93-94, 111-119
Laugardalslaug: 25
Laugar Spa: 25-26
Laugarvatn: 80-81
Laugarvatn Fontana: 80
Laugarvatn Swimming Pool: 80
Laugavegur: 6, 9, 11, 26, 32
Law Rock (Lögberg): 77-78
Laxness, Halldór: 57, 97, 120
Lennon, John: 65
LGBT travelers, tips for: 28, 30, 104
lighthouses: 70
Listasafn Íslands (National Gallery of
    Iceland): 10, 19
Listasafn Reykjavíkur (Reykjavík Art
    Museum): 7, 10, 11
literature: 96-97, 119-120
Ljósmyndasafn Reykjavíkur (Reykjavík
    Museum of Photography): 18-19
Lögberg (Law Rock): 77-78
lopapeysa sweater: 97
Lucky Records: 7, 34

M

Mál og Menning: 6, 33-34
maps: 12-13, 15, 58, 67, 77, 108
measurements: 110
medical services: 54, 106
metric system: 110
Mid-Atlantic Ridge: 76
midnight sun: 110
Mjodd station: 55
mobile phones: 108-109
Mokka: 7, 51
money: 93, 107-108
Mosfellsbær: 57-60
Mount Esja: 10, 57-59
Mount Syðstasúla: 79
music: 28-29, 30, 31, 34-35, 96

N

names: 94-95
National Gallery of Iceland (Listasafn
    Íslands): 10, 19
National Museum of Iceland
    (Þjóðminjasafn Íslands): 18
National Theater of Iceland
    (Þjóðleikhúsið): 29
NATO base: 66, 90, 91-92
Náttúrúfræðistofa (Natural History
    Museum): 61
newspapers: 53, 109-110

nightlife: *see* entertainment/events
Njarðvík: 66-69
Norræna Húsið (Nordic House): 18
northern lights: 22, 88-89

O

Ólafur Elíasson: 20
Ólafur Ragnar Grímsson: 91
Osushi: 7, 45, 64
outerwear: 105
Öxaráfoss: 78
Öxará River: 78
packing tips: 105

P

Parliament House (Alþingishúsið): 20
Parliament Plains (Þingvellir): 76
passports: 99
performing arts: 29
Perlan: 10, 23, 47
Pétursson, Hallgrímur: 16
pharmacies: 54, 106
phrasebook: 112-119
political parties: 91
pollution: 87-88
Pond, The (Tjörnin): 6, 10, 19-20
population: 93
pronunciation: 112-113
pylsur (hot dogs): 50, 102

QR

Raðhús (Reykjavík City Hall): 19
radio: 110
religion: 89, 95-96
rental cars: 55-56
restaurants: *see* food
Reykjanes Art Museum: 66
Reykjanesbær: 66-69
Reykjanes Folk Museum: 66
Reykjanes Maritime Center: 66-67
Reykjanes Peninsula: 66-75; map 67
Reykjavík Art Museum (Listasafn
    Reykjavíkur): 7, 10, 11
Reykjavík Arts Festival: 30, 94
Reykjavík Blues Festival: 30, 94
Reykjavík Botanical Garden
    (Grasagardur Reykjavíkur): 23
Reykjavík City Airport: 54, 55
Reykjavík City Hall (Raðhús): 19
Reykjavík Culture Night: 31, 95
Reykjavík Dance Festival: 30
Reykjavík Fashion Festival: 30
Reykjavík Food & Fun Festival: 31, 94
Reykjavík Grapevine: 53, 110, 120
Reykjavík International Film Festival: 31, 95
Reykjavík Jazz Festival: 30, 95

Reykjavík Museum of Photography (Ljósmyndasafn Reykjavíkur): 18-19
Reykjavík Pride: 30, 104
Reykjavík Zoo (Fjölskyldu- og Húsdýragarðinum): 22-23
rímur music: 96
RUV: 110

S
safety: 106-107
Saga Museum: 6, 18
sagas: *see* Icelandic Sagas
Saltfisksetur (Saltfish Museum): 72, 74
scuba diving: *see* diving
seasons: *see* climate
shoes: 105-106
shopping: 32-38, 108
Sigmundur Davið Gunnlaugsson: 91
Sinfóníuhljómsveit Íslands (Icelandic Symphony Orchestra): 29
Skólavörðustígur: 6, 7
skyr cheese: 48, 102
sleeping bag accommodations: 102
Smáralind: 38, 62
Snorri Sturluson: 97
Soley Natura Spa: 26
Sólfar (Sun Voyager): 10, 21-22
Sónar Reykjavík: 31, 94
Spark Design Space: 17
spas: 25-26, 71-72
sports/recreation: 24-26, 57-59, 78-79, 80; *see also specific place*
Strætó: 55
Strokkur: 82
Sturluson, Snorri: 97
Suðurbæjarlaug: 63
Sundhöllin: 25
Sun Voyager (Sólfar): 10, 21-22
surnames: 94-95
Sveinsson, Ásmundur: 14
swimming: 25, 59, 61, 63, 68, 73

T
taxes: 108
taxis: 54, 55
telephone services: 108-109
television: 110
Þingvallakirkja: 78
Þingvallavatn: 78
Þingvellir Interpretive Center: 76
Þingvellir National Park: 76-80
Þjóðleikhúsið (National Theater of Iceland): 29
Þjóðmenningarhúsið (Culture House): 16
Þjóðminjasafn Íslands (National Museum of Iceland): 18

Þorgeir Þorkelsson: 89
Þorkelsson, Þorgeir: 89
Þorrablót festival: 103
time zone: 110
tipping: 108
Tjörnin: 6, 10, 19-20
tourism: 92
tourist information: 53, 107, 120
transportation: 54-56, 100, 116-117; *see also specific place*
12 Tónar: 7, 34

UV
Varmárlaug: 59
VAT: 108
Vatnaveröld Swimming Pool: 68
Vesturbæjarlaug: 25
Viðeyjarstofa: 65
Viðey Island: 65
Vikingaheimar (Viking World): 67-68
Viking Festival: 63, 94-95
Viking Village (Fjörukráin): 63
Viking World (Vikingaheimar): 67-68
Vikin Maritime Museum: 22
visas: 99
volcanoes: 87

WXYZ
walking tours: 56
waterfalls: 78, 83-84, 88
water quality: 88, 103
weather: 86, 106
websites: 120-121
whales/whale-watching: 6, 24, 68
wheelchair accessibility: 104-105
Wi-Fi: 109
wildlife-watching: *see* bird-watching; whale-watching
women travelers, tips for: 103-104
World War II: 90

Þ
Þingvallakirkja: 78
Þingvallavatn: 78
Þingvellir Interpretive Center: 76
Þingvellir National Park: 76-80
Þjóðleikhúsið (National Theater of Iceland): 29
Þjóðmenningarhúsið (Culture House): 16
Þjóðminjasafn Íslands (National Museum of Iceland): 18
Þorgeir Þorkelsson: 89
Þorkelsson, Þorgeir: 89
Þorrablót festival: 103

INDEX

List of Maps

Central Reykjavík: 12–13
Downtown Reykjavík: 15
Greater Reykjavík: 58
Reykjanes Peninsula: 67
The Golden Circle: 77

Photo Credits

Also Available

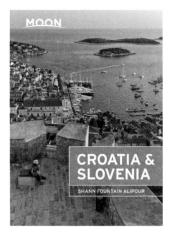

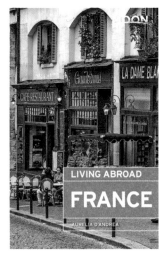

MAP SYMBOLS

Expressway	○ City/Town	✈ Airport	⚓ Golf Course
Primary Road	◉ State Capital	✗ Airfield	🅿 Parking Area
Secondary Road	◉ National Capital	▲ Mountain	⬤ Archaeological Site
Unpaved Road	★ Point of Interest	✛ Unique Natural Feature	♦ Church
Trail	• Accommodation		🅶 Gas Station
Ferry	▼ Restaurant/Bar	〰 Waterfall	Glacier
Railroad	■ Other Location	⚑ Park	Mangrove
Pedestrian Walkway		🚹 Trailhead	Reef
Stairs	▲ Campground	🎿 Skiing Area	Swamp

CONVERSION TABLES

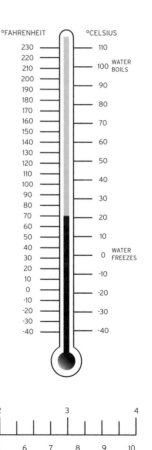

°C = (°F - 32) / 1.8
°F = (°C x 1.8) + 32
1 inch = 2.54 centimeters (cm)
1 foot = 0.304 meters (m)
1 yard = 0.914 meters
1 mile = 1.6093 kilometers (km)
1 km = 0.6214 miles
1 fathom = 1.8288 m
1 chain = 20.1168 m
1 furlong = 201.168 m
1 acre = 0.4047 hectares
1 sq km = 100 hectares
1 sq mile = 2.59 square km
1 ounce = 28.35 grams
1 pound = 0.4536 kilograms
1 short ton = 0.90718 metric ton
1 short ton = 2,000 pounds
1 long ton = 1.016 metric tons
1 long ton = 2,240 pounds
1 metric ton = 1,000 kilograms
1 quart = 0.94635 liters
1 US gallon = 3.7854 liters
1 Imperial gallon = 4.5459 liters
1 nautical mile = 1.852 km

MOON REYKJAVÍK
Avalon Travel
a member of the Perseus Books Group
1700 Fourth Street
Berkeley, CA 94710, USA
www.moon.com

Editor and Series Manager: Kathryn Ettinger
Copy Editor: Deana Shields
Graphics Coordinator: Elizabeth Jang
Production Coordinator: Darren Alessi
Cover Design: Faceout Studios, Charles Brock
Interior Design: Domini Dragoone
Moon Logo: Tim McGrath
Map Editor: Kat Bennett
Cartographers: Lohnes + Wright, Brian Shotwell, Kat Bennett
Indexer: Deana Shields

ISBN-13: 978-1-63121-514-8
ISSN: 2471-5433

Printing History
1st Edition — June 2016
5 4 3 2 1

JOSH likes art class and phys. ed., prefers his grubby jeans to his Sunday best . . . and gets around in a wheelchair.

AIMEE rides a scooter, baby-sits her younger brothers, has a dog named Scrappy . . . and is blind.

JAMIE has curly brown hair, loves to play charades . . . and can only ''hear'' you by reading your lips.

These three kids may have some handicaps, but they don't want your sympathy—they just want to be friends. Once you get to know them, you may be surprised at how much you have in common!

MEET MY FRIENDS

JONI EARECKSON TADA

Chariot Books
David C. Cook Publishing Co.

Cumberland Presbyterian Church
Dyersburg, Tennessee

Design and cover illustration by Dawn Lauck

First printing, 1987
Printed in the United States of America
91 90 89 88 87   1 2 3 4 5

Library of Congress Cataloging-in-Publication Data

Tada, Joni Eareckson.
  Meet my friends.

  "Chariot books."
  Summary: In this collection of three stories, young Christians find the strength to
overcome their physical handicaps.
  1. Children's stories, American. [1. Physically handicapped—Fiction. 2.
Christian life—Fiction. 3. Short stories] I. Durrell, Julie, ill. II. Title.
PZ7.T116Me 1987   [Fic]   8722344
ISBN 1-55513-808-X

When I was your age, I didn't know anyone in a wheelchair. I didn't know anyone who was blind. And the only person I knew who had a hearing problem was my Uncle Dick—and even that I hardly noticed, unless he forgot to wear his hearing aid.

The only time I ever saw a disabled person was when Mom and I would go shopping downtown on a bus. On the corner of Howard Street, a blind man always sat on a stool with a cup of pencils in his hand. His coat was tattered, and he had a collie beside him who looked like he wanted to be petted. I felt sorry for the blind man. In fact, I felt bad for all the disabled people I had never even met!

But then everything changed. Suddenly, I was the one in a wheelchair, as a result of breaking my neck after diving into shallow water. At first I was scared and lonely. I was afraid that people would feel sorry for me, just as I had felt sorry for the blind man on Howard Street.

But God changed everything. When I

put my life in His hands, I no longer felt scared and lonely. Jesus became my very best Friend, and He introduced me to a lot of other friends—some disabled like me and others on their feet like you. I was glad to learn that being in a wheelchair was nothing to be sorry about. It was the start of a new and exciting adventure.

While on this adventure, I've met so many special friends. I'd like to introduce you to a few of them. The kids you will meet in this book are not made up. The events which happened to them are not pretend. Three of them—Kristen, Camille, and Aimee—are grown-ups now, and we work and play together a lot. Their real-life stories are the inspiration for the children you will get to know here.

You'll find that Aimee, Josh, and Jamie are a lot like you. They have fights with their little brothers, want to be liked by their classmates, wear faded Levis, and love God.

So let's begin right now, because I want you to Meet My Friends!

THE IRON MAN

The alarm blasted and I fumbled for the off button. As soon as peace and quiet settled over my bedroom, I moaned and sank back into my pillow. It was the beginning of the second yucky week at my new school, Hillcrest Elementary. *I wish I were back at my old school,* I fumed, throwing back my covers, *with my old friends in my old fifth-grade class!*

Before I had my pajama top unbuttoned, Mom was in the room, gathering my shirt and pants from the closet.

"Mom, please . . . not those icky pants I wear to church. I want to wear my jeans. The real faded ones.''

"Joshie, not again! You've worn those jeans three days in a row.'' Mom rummaged through the pile of shirts, sweats, and underwear I'd stuffed in the corner. ''And how many times have I told you to put your dirty things in the hamper?''

Moms—they're always telling kids to pick up this and put away that. And they're always making up cutesy weird names like ''Joshie.'' I wish she'd just call me Josh like all my old friends.

''Do you want to wear your new Reeboks?'' she interrupted my thoughts.

''Nah. Tommy hasn't had a chance to get them nice and dirty yet.'' My brother, Tommy, is not your average stick-in-the-mud little brother. Actually, he is a neat little guy, especially when it comes to helping me break in a new stiff pair of jeans or scuff up a pair of tennis shoes so the soles will look walked on. Oh, yeah, I should explain—I'm in a wheelchair. Surprised? Well, don't let it hang you up.

8

I've been in a wheelchair since I was a little kid, and it's really not that bad. That is, as long as I've got friends who understand. Which brings me back to Hillcrest Elementary School.

Tommy and I chowed down breakfast and headed out the door. Tommy could have taken the bus, but he decided to ride with me in Mom's car. Like I said, Tommy's not bad for a third grader.

While Tommy finished his spelling homework, I doodled on my book covers. Mom, as usual, talked the whole way to school. Was my teacher assigning kids to help me? Did I have enough help during lunch? Was my classroom accessible? I don't know why she worries so much; I'm not a little kid anymore. And I can handle life—even fifth grade—in a wheelchair.

"—and are you making new friends, Joshie?"

I knew it would make her worry more, but I decided to be straight with her.

"Mom, you don't know what it's like at Hillcrest. I've been there a week, and I still don't know anybody. I hate being the new kid!'' Right away, I wished I hadn't told her. Now she would baby me.

But Mom did something that really surprised me. She didn't say anything. Finally, Mom spoke, but in a different tone.

''Joshua, we can't help it that Daddy's work brought us to a new neighborhood. Remember our prayers last night?''

I nodded. It had felt good to pray.

''We asked God for new friends at Hillcrest. And we asked Him to help you to be brave.''

Mom was right. I did pray those things. But as we pulled up to the front of Hillcrest Elementary, I didn't feel too courageous. Tommy helped unfold my wheelchair, waved, and ran off to his class. There it sat, my new zippy sports chair—black and chrome—gleaming in the sun. It had a low-slung, leather back, new super ball bearings on the racing wheels, and black, foam grips on the handles. With orange flame decals on the

10

sides, it looked more like a supermodified formula racer. I didn't care what anybody thought—I was proud of my wheels!

Mom grabbed the waistband of my jeans and hiked me out of the car and into the wheelchair. She did some nice "mother things" like roll up the cuffs of my jeans and loosely lace my shoestrings the way the other kids did.

"Mom, I'm sorry. I don't mean to make you worry. It's just that, well. . . . There's a girl in my class who wears braces, and they call her Tinsel-Teeth Tammy." I grabbed hold of the metal rim of my wheels. "Who knows what jerky name they'll come up with for me?"

Mom did what she always does when we have these honest talks about my disability. She knelt by my wheels and stroked my hair like she did when I was a baby. "Mo-o-om!" I put on a whine, glad that Tommy wasn't around to see. But it did feel good.

I jostled around on my seat cushion to get comfortable, piled my books on my lap, slung my duffel bag over the handle of my chair, and started off. With a hard shove, my chair and I coasted down the ramp to the school entrance. Putting on my bravest smile for the kids hanging around the flagpole, I recognized one of the boys from my class. Johnson—I didn't know if it was his last name or a nickname. But there was no chance to ask. The kids broke up and walked away as I came near. I was hoping Johnson would hold the front door open for me, but he disappeared by the time I got there. It was a good thing Mom had decided to visit the school office; she caught up with me and held open the door. I wheeled into the noisy, crowded foyer.

"Bye," I called and turned my wheelchair toward the hallway. The smile on Mom's face was one that meant: "Josh, you know I would like to help." She always felt that way. But our family was used to letting me face my own problems, even though I was still a kid.

My wheels made squeaky sounds on

the shiny linoleum and a couple of boys
carrying backpacks turned around to look
at me. I flashed them a smile, but they
only moved aside to give me passing
room. Then I noticed that half the kids in
the hallway had parted like the Red Sea. I
felt six feet wide.

"Watch out for your toes, guys," I
teased as I glided past the boys with
backpacks. I hoped they'd chuckle back,
but nobody said anything to me. There

was just the usual before-school chatter about skateboards and Atari games and what was on the Disney Sunday movie the night before.

I got to class early and pushed aside a couple of empty desks to get to my place. I stacked my books—Dad had helped Tommy and me cover our books with brown, paper grocery bags over the weekend. That's what the kids did at Hillcrest, and we wanted to fit in. I reached into my duffel bag and pulled out my homework on diagramming sentences. As I was going over my work, I noticed Johnson waltz in, cracking gum and shuffling baseball cards. He wadded his gum and tossed a sky hook toward the wastebasket. Instead it hit Tammy's desk.

''Sorry, Tinsel-Teeth. Must be those magnets in your mouth,'' Johnson said flippantly as he picked his gum off her desk. I felt really bad for her.

For a second, I thought he looked my way. I smiled, but he quickly flopped into his seat with his back to me. I sighed,

14

grabbed my pencils, and began wheeling toward the line at the sharpener in the back of the room.

"Oh, let me get out of your way," a girl in a sweat shirt and high-topped tennis shoes said, stepping aside.

"Hey, no problem. You're fine where you are," I answered. But I think she was afraid to look at me. She just kept talking real fast to her friend who was wearing the same kind of sweat shirt and tennis shoes. *Girls,* I thought. *All they care about is stupid photographs of TV stars and Barbie dolls—and each other.* The morning was off to a winner of a start. I decided I wouldn't say anything else in line.

Most of the day was yucky—just like the week before. I did everything everyone else did: I wheeled my chair up front to write on the blackboard, I was able to fit down the aisles to help pass out papers, I could reach for the plants by the windowsill to help water them. I even tried to share my chocolate chip cookies, but only one kid took them, and he acted like the cookies had cooties. I pulled out my G. I. Joes and matchbox cars from my duffel bag during recess, but all the other guys wanted to play dodge ball. I tried to crack a few jokes, but no one really thought they were funny. Except for one person. . . .

It was during lunch. A boy named Harold (and that's what everybody called him, not Hal or Harry, but Harold) was asked by our teacher to carry my lunch tray from the cafeteria line to the table. I hadn't noticed him much in class, except that the rest of the kids enjoyed picking on him. I guess that's because Harold got lots of A's, especially in science. He was interested in dinosaurs and carried a picture of a Tyrannosaurus Rex in his wallet. He drew pictures of the solar system on his book covers and always laced his tennis shoes up tight instead of leaving them undone.

But I liked him. I don't know, maybe I felt sorry for him, too. I guess getting

16

picked on is a lot worse than being ignored. Besides, Harold seemed genuinely glad to carry my tray, even though he was assigned the job.

Could Harold be God's answer to prayer for a good friend at Hillcrest? Naah! At least, I hoped not. I wasn't sure I wanted to hang around Harold too much—I might get picked on, too. But it *was* nice to have someone to talk to. And as I said, he liked my jokes.

"Hey, Harold," I said as I slapped the seat next to me, inviting him to sit and eat his lunch. "You know what they say about my wheelchair?"

Harold bit into his sandwich and shook his head no.

"I'm into heavy metal."

Harold laughed so hard he spit bologna and lettuce all over the table. I thought I might like him after all.

"So what's with the other guys?" I reached in my lunch bag for what was left of my chocolate chip cookies. "Nobody seems to want to make friends around here." I looked at the empty seats near us and then at the crowded tables around the rest of the cafeteria.

"It's not so bad," Harold said with his sandwich in his mouth again. "At least we're always guaranteed a place to sit at lunch."

I threw my last cookie back in my bag along with the rest of my trash. "Forget it. Kids in this school act like they've never seen a wheelchair before."

Harold took a long time, chewing and thinking. "You, at least, they ignore. Me, they pick on." He paused again. "I think most kids just feel they need to pick on somebody."

I thought of Tinsel-Teeth Tammy and looked at Harold as he wiped his mouth with the back of his hand. "Who made up that rule?" I muttered as I unlocked the brakes to my chair.

We finished lunch and lined up with the rest of the class to head for art. Of all the things about Hillcrest school, I liked art and phys. ed. the best. Mrs. DePesto

18

made art so much fun. Today we were going to design posters for next week's Junior Olympics.

"Hey, need a push?" I heard a girl say behind Harold and me. I looked over my shoulder and saw a blonde-haired girl with a single long braid. I knew that her friends—the girls in sweat shirts and tennis shoes—called her Kerrie. But she wasn't like the other dumb girls; she acted more like a guy. I liked her.

In art class, Mrs. DePesto divided us up into groups of three to work on Junior Olympics posters. I didn't say it, but I was glad that Kerrie was assigned to work with Harold and me. In no time we had paste, colored paper, poster paints, and glitter everywhere.

"How about this for a poster title—'Make Tracks for the Junior Olympics!'?" I suggested.

"Uh . . . sure," Kerrie said. "But I don't get it."

"Me, neither," chipped in Harold.

"You'll see," I said with a sly grin.

"Harold, hand me a brush. Kerrie, lift that paint can up here, will you?" They shrugged their shoulders at each other and followed through. I dipped my brush deep into the paint and began slapping the color on my wheels.

They looked at me as though I had bananas for brains.

Then, "He-e-ey," said Harold, as though a light bulb had gone on over his head. "I get the idea!" He and Kerrie grabbed brushes and began to carefully cover every inch of tread on my wheels.

Kerrie spread sheets of poster board in front of and behind my chair. "Okay, I'll get in the front. Harold, you grab the back." Kerrie pulled while Harold pushed. I leaned over to catch a look. Bright red tracks silk-screened a bunch of tire tread patterns on yellow poster board. They pushed and pulled my wheelchair over five other sheets of board, each a different color.

"All right!" Harold exclaimed, wiping his hands on his pants.

"Not bad," Kerrie said, as she let out a low whistle.

The rest of the class had put down their scissors and paste to see what we were up to. Thankfully, Mrs. DePesto thought our posters were tops. I could tell that most of the other kids were impressed, too. All except Johnson and his buddies—it was plain they weren't interested in posters of Junior Olympics.

When the 3:30 bell rang, Tommy and I were out on the curb, waiting for Mom. I didn't see Kerrie or Harold anywhere. I had wanted to tell them thanks for being such good sports in art class, and for, well . . . being *almost* friends.

That night, Tommy jabbered on and on at the dinner table about the snake his friend brought in for show and tell. I decided to keep my art class triumph to myself for the time being. Fifth grade was beginning to look a little brighter at Hillcrest Elementary, but there was still a long way to go.

On the way to school the next day,

Mom hardly had a chance to get a word in edgewise. Tommy and I traded stories about our teachers, the cafeteria food, recess, and the Junior Olympics. I could tell Mom was relieved *not* to hear whining.

At lunchtime, Harold was there again to help me carry my tray. We had a lot to talk about—where the posters should be hung and which Junior Olympic events we should try out for.

After lunch we lined up as usual. Today was my other favorite class—phys. ed. Coach Brubaker would be testing our entire class for next week's Olympics. We'd be competing with kids from Milford Elementary School in events like the hundred-yard dash, the softball throw, and the long jump.

"Hey, Harold," yelled one of the boys from the back of the line, "maybe Coach Brubaker has an event just for you—the dinosaur dash!"

Here we go again! I groaned to myself.

"Stegasaurus, Brontosaurus,

Tyrannosaurus Rex—Harold smells as gross as a dinosaur's breath."

"Back off, Johnson," I heard a girl say behind us. I looked over my shoulder and saw Kerrie holding a softball and glove. For a second I thought I saw her smile at Harold and me, but maybe she was only cracking gum. I turned around and began wheeling my chair, following the rest of the kids to phys. ed. I liked Kerrie. She stood up for Harold even when I couldn't—or, should I say, didn't.

Outside on the playground, Coach Brubaker separated us into groups. A few kids went to the track to be tested, and others, including Kerrie, headed for the softball diamond. I parked my wheelchair under the basketball net, leaned over to pick up a ball, and began turning it over in my hands while waiting for Coach to decide what to do with me.

"Harold, you'll stay in this group." Coach Brubaker pointed with his whistle toward me and a few others who were hanging around under the net. Looking at the others, I realized our group was made up of kids who weren't very good at sports. I was always getting stuck with kids who weren't athletic, but that didn't bother me. Coach Brubaker had no way of knowing how strong I was or how well I could dribble or shoot a basket—or even how fast I could wheel my chair.

I gave Harold a big grin. We were becoming a regular duo. I bounced the ball to him.

Coach Brubaker made each of us stand behind the foul line and shoot baskets. He was really surprised when I made eight out of my ten tries. Harold, on the other hand, couldn't make even one. He stuffed his hands in his pockets and kicked at the blacktop.

Just then Johnson and some of his buddies walked by the basketball court on their way in from the track. "Hey, Harold, why don't you try standing on a ladder . . . even you can make baskets that way!" They held their sides, doubling over in laughter.

24

I didn't see what was so funny. Feeling my face get red, I knew I had to get away from there before I exploded. Without thinking, I gave my wheels a hard shove and raced toward a basketball. As my chair whizzed by it, I stretched to reach for the ball. "Oh, no . . ." I felt my wheelchair tip. I was falling.

Crash!!

"Help! Coach Brubaker!" I could hear Harold yelling.

Nobody was laughing anymore. Instead, I could feel their eyes on me. I knew I wasn't hurt, or at least I didn't think I was. Falls like these have happened a lot.

"Joshua, are you all right?" Coach Brubaker said as he helped me sit up. "Harold, go get Josh's chair."

"Aaaaw." I rubbed my elbow and glanced at the kids standing around. A few turned their backs. Some pretended nothing happened. Johnson just stared. It dawned on me that they were more embarrassed than I was. I not only felt embarrassed, I felt sick. And suddenly, I felt angry. Not at the kids so much. I was angry at my paralyzed legs. And I was angry at God.

"Here, let me," Harold said as he locked the brakes on my wheelchair and grabbed my legs. He and Coach Brubaker helped me back into my seat. Their smiles made me feel a lot better.

"Those . . . those bean brains," Harold grumbled, casting an angry glance at Johnson, who was dribbling a basketball with his buddies at the other end of the court. "Who needs them?"

I knew exactly what Harold was feeling. I had felt like that zillions of times, for as long as I could remember. But being angry at other kids just because they tease you or, in my case, ignore you, just doesn't cut it. Also, I had learned that feeling down on myself or God got me nowhere. I sighed deeply. I had to come up with a whole new plan of action.

"Harold, we are not going to give up," I said, as I wiped the dirt off my hands.

"Huh?" Harold looked blank.

"Coach Brubaker," I said. "I've got an idea!"

The next day our teacher gave her okay. For the next few days Coach Brubaker came to get Harold and me out of class early.

"Hey, where are you guys going?" Kerrie whispered, as I wheeled past her desk toward the door. I smiled at her. I wished I could let her in on our secret, but Harold and Coach and I had agreed. It would be a surprise.

"How come they get out early?" Johnson sneered.

"Yeah, what's going on?" a couple of others demanded.

No way was I going to give a clue. I plopped my books on my lap and buzzed out the door with my best smug look. After Coach clicked shut the classroom door behind us, Harold and I let out a whoop and headed for the gymnasium.

• • •

The day of the Junior Olympics finally

arrived. Bright and early, several buses from Milford Elementary pulled up to the front of Hillcrest. Kids piled out of the buses with their softball bats and gloves, track shoes, school banners, and lunch bags. As our school bell rang, kids from every class poured out the doors and organized into teams on the field. Johnson and his buddies headed for the track. I gave the thumbs-up sign to Kerrie, who headed for the softball diamond with her ball and glove. I whipped my chair around; kids were cheering everywhere. For the first time in weeks I began to feel a little bit of Hillcrest school spirit.

Coach Brubaker handed Harold and me stopwatches and clipboards. "You boys know what to do, right? Make certain that the boys and girls who are competing are properly listed. Write down their numbers. Get their accurate times. Okay?" He checked off a list on his clipboard. "You boys will make good statisticians."

"Stati-what?" I said, squinting.

"Just ask Harold," Coach smiled.

Harold was deep in paperwork. He kept pushing his glasses back on his nose with one hand and scribbling names and events while balancing a clipboard on his lap with the other. Numbers and figures. He was right at home with his job.

I draped a whistle around my neck and pulled down a visor over my eyes. "Ready?" I called to Harold as I stuffed the event sheets in my duffel bag and wheeled toward the playground.

"Ready!" he said as he gathered his papers and followed, giving the leather back of my wheelchair a slap.

We wheeled over to the long jump area, watched the competition, and collected the results. Milford won that event. The sun was getting high in the sky as we headed for the softball diamond to check out the game. Hillcrest was ahead by two runs. The tension was high as the two schools split for lunch.

Next were the track events. Milford ran away with the high jump. Hillcrest topped the hurdles. The results so far were split down the middle. We watched Kerrie win the softball throw. Harold and I quickly compared our numbers—her win put Hillcrest ahead by one event. But Johnson didn't win the hundred-yard dash as he hoped—and Milford and Hillcrest were now tied.

"Way to go," Harold muttered at Johnson who was bending over, still wheezing.

"Well, let's see you get on the track and do better, Mr. Stupid-Scorekeeper," Johnson spat back.

"Oh, yeah?"

"Hey, lighten up." I jabbed Harold good-naturedly in the side.

"Well, he's always—"

"Doesn't matter." I lowered my voice. "We're in this together, okay?"

Harold adjusted his glasses as he adjusted his attitude. I didn't mean to scold him. It's just that I had tried that old trick of giving others a taste of their own medicine. It always backfired. But now, something *was* about to work, and work big! It was time for our secret plan!

"Okay, you two." Coach Brubaker herded us toward the chin-up bar on the playground. "Josh, your event is the next and last."

"Josh has an event?" Kerrie asked, surprised.

"But he's a . . . a handicap," one of Johnson's friends protested.

I handed over my whistle and visor to Kerrie. She didn't say anything, just smiled and gave me her thumbs-up sign.

Milford and Hillcrest kids parted to let us through. This time it felt kind of good to imagine myself six feet wide.

"Coming through. Stand back, everyone." Harold played the role of a playground monitor.

I gave my sports chair a big shove and coasted past the assembled classes.

"Come on, Hillcrest, three cheers for Josh!" I heard Kerrie yell behind me. A couple of kids whooped and hollered. But neither she nor the rest of my classmates

really knew what was up. I hoped I would be able to pull it off!

I stopped short of the chin-up bar. Milford's top kid was already on his fifth chin-up. I kneaded the muscles in my hands as I watched the muscular boy strain toward ten chin-ups.

Milford began to get rowdy. "Come on! Hang in there! Go for it!"

The Milford boy began to shake as he sweated and jerked toward twelve.

"Keep going! Keep going!" A couple of kids waved banners and flags.

Thirteen.

Fourteen.

The boy let out a groan as his chin crested the bar for the fifteenth time. He dropped to the sand, exhausted. Immediately he was surrounded by his cheering friends. He had tied the Junior Olympic record for the fifth grade.

"Good going," I said as I stretched my hand toward him with a broad smile.

He wiped his hands on a towel and confidently stretched his hand toward me. I couldn't help but be amazed at the natural way he returned my handshake. Here he was a stranger, and yet he accepted me right off. My own classmates didn't even do that.

The moment was over too quickly. It was my turn.

"Give him room; give him room." Coach spread his hands as Harold helped me position my chair directly underneath the chin-up bar.

"Ready?" Harold rubbed his hands together.

I took a deep breath, squinted shut my eyes, and prayed silently. *Please, God, help me not to be a show-off. You've given me strong arms to push a chair. Now let these arms show the kids the gift You've given me. And, er, it would be nice to win. Uh, that is, I mean . . . win new friends.*

I opened my eyes. There was my little brother Tommy. He had squeezed his way through the crowd to the edge of the sand. I gave him a wink. He tried his way of winking back—blinking both eyes.

I rubbed my sweaty palms on my jeans. Harold and Coach Brubaker hoisted me out of my chair and held me still until I could grab the bar tightly. "Ready!" I said, and they let go. Immediately I felt the weight of my paralyzed legs pull me down. The muscles in my arms stretched.

With a mighty heave, I flexed. My body rose and I completed my first chin-up. I heard a smattering of applause from the Hillcrest kids. Although my legs hung limp, my upper body twisted as I kept chinning quickly up to number eight. From then on, it was going to be a real contest.

"Number nine!" a couple of Hillcrest kids began to chant.

I felt the years of pushing my wheelchair begin to pay off. "Number ten!" the chant spread throughout the Hillcrest crowd.

"Number eleven!" Tammy didn't seem to care about spitting through her braces every time she cheered. "Number twelve!" I relaxed for a moment, letting my body weight stretch my arms. My hands burned. My shoulders ached. Sweating and straining, I continued. "Number thirteen!" I heard Tommy screech. *Thanks, God!* I said to myself as I felt the cold metal of the bar underneath my chin again.

"Come on, Josh!" Kerrie jumped up and down. Suddenly I felt a surge of energy. My pace quickened. "Number fourteen—fifteen—Josh has got the Junior Olympic record tied!'' Hillcrest kids were wild with excitement.

"He's going for an all-class record." Coach Brubaker looked at his clipboard. "Sixteen—seventeen!"

My smile expanded and I almost giggled. I was about to surprise everyone, including myself. "Eighteen—nineteen!" By this time even Milford was cheering me on. The kids were jumping up and down in a frenzy.

"Twenty chin-ups . . . a state record!" Coach Brubaker threw his visor in the air, and a tremendous cheer went up from the entire playground. Kerrie was doing cartwheels. Harold and Tammy were actually hugging each other.

My fists felt frozen to the bar. "Hey, you guys, somebody get me down," I managed between gasps. Immediately Harold and Coach wrapped their arms around my knees and lowered me to my chair as though it were a king's throne. It felt so good to sit down!

As I blew on my hot hands, somebody handed me a towel. I smashed my sweaty face into it; then I looked up. Johnson.

"You're pretty tough," he said with a cocky smile. "You're a real iron man."

"Hey, yeah, Iron Man," Harold said, slapping me a high five.

A nickname . . . an honest to goodness nickname—besides Joshie.

"Hey, Iron Man," someone shouted from the middle of the crowd, "where'd you learn to chin-up like that?"

"My coach—Coach Hal. Right, Hal?" I grinned and winked at Harold, who stood there a little dumbfounded. Coach Brubaker crooked his arm around Hal's neck and tousled his hair.

"Not bad, Hal," Johnson said. "You're not as nerdy as I thought."

Hal blushed.

The crowd began to thin as kids headed for the awards ceremony in front of the bleachers by the softball diamond. We had won the Junior Olympic trophy.

I let my little brother push me to the

softball field. Harold carried my duffel bag, and Kerrie strolled beside me.

"Next thing you know, the guys will be lining up a mile deep to arm wrestle you," she said.

I chuckled. "Iron Man. Hmmm . . . Feels nice to be accepted."

"You think it was just because of your chin-ups?" Kerrie asked.

I gave her the sort of knowing smile I had often seen my mom give me. I knew the inside story. Everybody—Tammy, Coach Brubaker, even Johnson—felt better about seeing not only me in a new light, but Harold, too. It had become cool *not* to pick on somebody. Or to ignore.

I gathered Tommy in my arms and hoisted him up on my lap. With a hard shove, we went careening down the path to the softball field. The cool, late afternoon air rushed through my hair. I leaned my head back and breathed a sigh of relief. *Thanks God—You did it. Answered prayers and more friends than I can count!*

FRIENDS ON CANWOOD STREET

My name is Aimee and I live on Canwood Street, the most beautiful street in town. It's especially nice this time of year—the oak trees are full of leaves, and the weather is warm enough to ride my scooter. Mrs. Gardner, four doors up, has roses growing over her picket fence, and Mr. Espey, next door, always gives our family a bag of his home-grown tomatoes. Canwood Street is a perfect place to live—except for Grandpa Dudley across the street.

Grandpa Dudley isn't really my grandpa, but Mom told me to call him that out of politeness. He's nice enough, I suppose, but there are times when I don't feel like being very polite to him. Like this morning . . .

"Hi, there, Aimee!" Grandpa Dudley called as he raked leaves in his front yard. I stopped my scooter at his curb. "You sure do ride that thing well for a handicapped girl."

"Yeah," I mumbled as I swiveled my handlebars.

That's what I didn't like about Grandpa Dudley. He always called me "handicapped." Handicapped people use wheelchairs or are retarded. And I am *not* in a wheelchair, nor am I retarded. I felt like telling that to Grandpa Dudley.

I heard the scratch of his rake, and I knew he had gone back to his yard work. I listened carefully for cars and then gave my scooter a shove. I coasted across the street to our house, where I knew Mom was in the backyard hanging laundry.

"Mom," I said, as I leaned my scooter up against our fence, "do you think I'm handicapped?"

I could tell she was shaking out damp towels; they smelled so wet and fresh.

"Well, yes and no, Aimee. You are handicapped when people don't let you do things you know you *can* do." She stopped, probably to think for a minute. "You're handicapped when your teachers forget to . . . let's say, type your papers in Braille. But for the most part, honey, I don't think of you as handicapped. And neither do Daddy or your little brothers."

Mom drew me close against her apron

and gave me a big squeeze.

I rubbed my eyes as she held me in her arms. I know you're going to think this is strange, but my eyes aren't like yours— they're made of glass. But you would never know; in fact, they never look tired or red and are a pretty color of blue, my mother tells me.

Mom went back to her laundry, and I sat on the back porch steps with Scrappy, my scruffy-looking gray-haired dog. I love Scrappy—he licks my cheek whenever I feel sad. And I was never sadder than when I lost my eyesight because of something called *retinal blastoma*. Scrappy came to live with us then. I may have lost my sight, but I was glad I got him. Maybe one day he'll be my guide dog.

I held Scrappy for a long time, thinking about what Mom had said. "I don't care what Grandpa Dudley thinks," I whispered into Scrappy's ear. "I am *not* handicapped. Oh, I crash into my fair share of trees and poles when I'm not paying attention, but I can roller-skate and ride my scooter like most kids.''

I turned Scrappy's face toward me. Stroking his forehead, I continued, ''Somebody just has to show me the street a few times, and I'm on my own. I can even feel if there's a parked car in the way.'' I stopped for a minute. *''Except* if it's a windy day, or if I have a cold. Then I don't have very good balance. Scrappy, what do you think? Does that makes me handicapped?''

He licked my cheek, just as I knew he would.

The next day I gathered my papers for my science report and left early for school. I've walked to school a hundred times before, and I know every crack in the sidewalk. Maybe I was handicapped when I was first learning the way, tripping and stumbling. But after running into the fire hydrant at the corner of Canwood and Oak a few times, I'm a lot more careful. I even know where Mrs. Gardner's thorny rosebush sticks out over the fence. *I-AM-NOT . . . HAN-DI-CAPPED,* I repeated to myself, keeping a rhythm as I walked.

The school halls were really crowded, and I had to concentrate hard to use my "radar" so I wouldn't bump into anyone. I better explain that—my "radar" (or facial vision, as my doctor calls it) helps me feel when something is near me. That's how I can find my seat in the classroom, walk around a telephone pole on the way home, or even swerve to avoid Mrs. Gardner's bushes. Last year in the third grade I tried using a cane, but I decided I didn't need it. People say I have unusually good radar. Maybe that's because I lost my sight when I was a little kid instead of a baby.

I made it to my classroom with minutes to spare.

"Hi, Aimee," Judy called from her seat. Judy is my best friend. By the echo in her voice, I could tell our classroom was still mostly empty. I waved hello in her direction.

44

"Are you ready to give your report today, Aimee?" Mrs. Collins asked as she was writing on the chalkboard.

"I sure am, Mrs. Collins," I said as I placed my duffel bag by my desk and felt for my chair. I like my teacher a lot. She and the teacher's aide type a lot of my assignments in Braille—little bumps in patterns on plain white pages. I run my fingers over the bumps and can feel each word. My books are big and bulky compared to the nice, small books my classmates use. When I walk down the hall, I always carry my books in a duffel bag so no one will see how big they are.

Mrs. Collins likes me so much it's a little embarrassing. I don't want her treating me special in front of the other kids. I have to admit it is nice, though, when she lets me pass out papers, water the plants, or help put up bulletin boards. Sometimes when she loses things on the floor—little things like paper clips or pins—I help her find them. My fingers are totally sensitive. But speaking of sensitive things, there's one person in my class who is anything but. . . .

"Hey, Aimee, who dressed you this morning? You have on one pink sock and one brown!" That was weirdo Alan.

"Alan, that will be enough," Mrs. Collins said sternly.

Dumb Alan. He was always trying to trick me into thinking my blouse was polka-dotted and my skirt was striped. As usual, I knew he was wrong. I had checked my socks before I put them on this morning—I could tell by feeling if I had the right ones. But just to double-check, I reached down to feel once more, pretending to scratch my ankle.

Later that morning, during our science unit, it was time to give my report on clouds. I gathered my duffel bag and notes and slowly made my way to the front of the class. I was so nervous that I wasn't paying attention and ran into Jared's desk. I heard snickering from the direction of Alan's seat. But I felt better once I was holding on to the podium. Mrs.

Collins helped me spread out my notes.

Running my fingers nervously over the pages, I looked straight ahead and delivered my speech about the differences between cumulus, cirrus, and stratus clouds. I read a quote about cloud seeding from my Braille science book— underlined with staples so I could find it easily. Then I pulled out a wad of cotton balls from my duffel bag.

"I think clouds must look so soft and fluffy, that if we could touch them, they might feel like this." I passed handfuls of cotton balls down each row. "Close your eyes and imagine what you have in your hands is part of a real thunderhead," I instructed the class.

The room was quiet while each student slowly handled the cotton.

"Wow . . . Yeah . . ." a couple of kids said. I breathed a big sigh of relief. My report was over.

As I sat down and the next student began to give his report, I heard someone behind me say, "Pssst."

A note was shoved into my hand. I ran my fingers over the underside of the paper and felt the impression of the hard-penciled words.

Your report was neat!
Love,
Judy

Judy and most of the kids in class were my very good pals. All except weirdo Alan. I was getting tired of his stupid jokes. Yesterday when I brought my Braille spell writer into class to take notes, he had something smart to say.

"Yikes . . . what's *that* thing?"

"It's a bomb!" I snapped back at him. "If you don't watch it, I'll set it off and blow you to smithereens, Alan!"

At recess that afternoon it got worse. My girl friends and I were minding our own business, playing Old Maid with my Braille cards. After we finished, Alan came up and scared me, yelling that I was about to step into a hole. I was embarrassed, until Judy told me it was

48

just another one of his jokes.

That did it! I felt like taking out my glass eyes and throwing them at him! Instead, I shut my eyes tightly and tried to hold back the tears.

As we lined up to leave the playground, I still felt like crying. Why were Alan and his stupid pranks upsetting me so? I nudged Judy. "Do you think I'm . . . handicapped?"

Judy didn't say anything for a while. When the line began to move, she spoke up. "Aimee, I'm not sure what that means. You don't wear hearing aids or crutches. You're not like a poster kid on a telethon, if that's what you mean."

Good old Judy. I was relieved that she didn't think I was handicapped.

After school I headed home, stopping to smell Mrs. Gardner's roses. Scrappy came running to meet me—I could tell it was Scrappy by the jingle of his collar. Just as I was about to turn into our driveway, I heard Grandpa Dudley call from across the street. "Hi, there, Aimee!

Your mom said to tell you she had to run to the store. Do you need any help getting into the house?''

I fumed inside. "No, that's okay."

If I couldn't change Alan's opinion of me, I was certainly going to change Grandpa Dudley's.

I let myself in the house, fixed some chocolate milk, and flicked on the TV. Mom arrived home after a short while, with Grandpa Dudley helping her carry in groceries.

"Aimee, would you mind baby-sitting Matt and Chris tonight? Dad called, and we have to go to a dinner meeting. We'll only be gone a couple hours."

Grandpa Dudley nearly dropped the bag of groceries. "Aimee? Baby-sitting by herself?"

I jerked open the refrigerator door and put the fruit juice and milk away. "I can *do* it, Grandpa. It's only for a couple of hours!"

I'm a *good* baby-sitter. I had helped change Matt and Chris's diapers, fed them, burped them, and put them to bed when they were babies. Now that they're five and six, the boys are used to my being blind. We three are a team.

"Aimee, I've never met a handicapped girl like you. You're amazing!" Grandpa clucked as he walked out the back door.

Thankfully, my mother didn't think I was "amazing." It was an accepted fact in my family that I could be put in charge of Matt and Chris for a couple of hours.

The boys were thrilled to learn I'd be baby-sitting—but it wasn't because they loved me. . . . They loved to *test* me. The games began as soon as Mom and Dad closed the front door behind them.

As I was putting away dinner dishes and getting ready to relax in the living room, I heard the faint click of the back door opening. "Matt, get back in here!"

I heard his little feet come running. "How'd you know, Aimee?" he whined.

I grabbed him and gave him a squeeze. "Because you and your little brother are so noisy. When are you going to learn to be quiet enough to fool me?'' I laughed. ''Remember the time you tried to sneak into my bedroom and change around my clothes so I would get confused?''

Matt giggled and squirmed.

''I caught you, didn't I?'' I said, tickling him. ''Okay, let's see how good you are. Chris?'' I looked toward the couch where I knew he was sitting, building with Legos. ''Are you ready to play our game?''

Chris hopped off the couch and ran toward Matt. The boys giggled and got ready. The air got still and then I could feel one of them put his hand up in front of my face. It was my job to guess how many stubby little fingers he was holding up.

''How many, Aimee?''

''Let's see . . . hmm . . . bring your hand a bit closer, Chris.'' I could feel the air move as his hand drew closer to my face. ''Three! You're holding up three.''

''How did you know?!'' Chris stomped his foot on the ground.

I leaned back on my heels and folded my arms. "I don't know, Chris. I can just, I don't know, feel the air," I said. I grinned at him.

"Do it again!" Matt said. We kept it up for ten minutes. I beat them fifteen out of twenty times.

"Hide-and-seek! Let's play hide-and-seek next!" They were determined to wear me out, but I was just as determined to keep up with them until Dad and Mom got home.

"Okay, now. Remember you can only use this room. One . . . two . . ." I counted up to ten while they scurried to find places to hide.

I have to admit that I loved playing hide-and-seek, too. It was a good test for my radar. And poor Matt and Chris! No matter how hard they tried, I could always hear them breathing behind a chair or catch the sound of their feet and hands rustling on the carpet.

"Where are you?" I called in a sing-song way. "Let's see . . . Where is

Chris?'' I turned around to begin walking to the other side of the living room. Instinctively, I knew that one of those little stinkers was standing right in the middle of the room, not even bothering to hide behind a chair!

''Gotcha!'' I reached out and grabbed a giggling little brother. Matt. After we played the game a few more times, we plopped down on the couch to watch TV. Just as we got settled, Chris decided he wanted chicken soup.

''Chicken soup? You just had dinner.'' I sighed, got up, and led him to the kitchen. ''I knew Mom should have made you finish your plate.''

I ran my hand over a few of the cans. Fruit cocktail cans were larger than soup cans. I shoved cans of tomato paste out of the way—they were smaller. I put my hand around one can of soup and held it up for Chris to see.

''Tell me the letters,'' I said. Sometimes I suspected that Chris was more interested in reading the letters than

he was in eating the soup.

"C-H-I. . . ." he said.

He didn't have to go any further. I
knew it wasn't chili—the can sloshed like
soup. Within minutes I had it opened and
the soup heating. I sat next to Chris,
watching him eat. Or, I should say,
listening to him slurp.

After he finished, I flipped back the
plastic crystal on my watch and read the
hands. Almost eight-thirty. Time for
Mom and Dad to be home soon, and time

for Chris and Matt to get ready for bed.

"A story! Please, Aimee, a story!" Brothers. I sat down on the love seat and gathered the boys close. They didn't think of me as handicapped. In fact, they thought my blindness was a neat thing. Like Mom and Dad, and even Scrappy, they loved me, with or without the ability to see.

I cuddled them and sang and made up stories until the two of them were fast asleep in my arms. I should have wakened them and put them to bed, but I knew our parents would be home any minute.

Just then I heard a key in the front door. When I felt Mom and Dad step through the front door, I raised a finger to my lips. "Sshhh."

"Everything go okay?" Dad asked as he lifted Chris off my lap.

I yawned and nodded, happy that, once again, I had been trusted to do things that I *knew* I could do.

The next morning I was up early for school. Gathering my books and patting

56

Matt and Chris on the head, I stepped out the front door with Scrappy. Halfway down our walk, I heard the scratch of Grandpa Dudley's rake across the street. I felt my watch and realized I had a few extra minutes. Listening for traffic, I walked across the street.

"Good morning, Grandpa," I called as I felt for the curb and slung my duffel bag over my shoulder. "You're getting an early start on your yard work."

"Got to get to it before the sun gets high and hot," he said as I sensed him draw nearer to the fence. "How'd the baby-sitting go?"

"Fine . . . as usual," I answered, trying not to sound sarcastic.

"Well, little girl, you are one amazing lady."

I sighed. In Grandpa's eyes, I was either too crippled to do anything for myself *or* I was Supergirl, the fantastic blind kid, not to be believed unless seen with your very own eyes.

I guess that's the way it will always be.

There will always be a weirdo Alan who
could care less. There will always be a
Grandpa Dudley who is amazed at
whatever I do. And there will always be a
Matt and Chris who don't seem to know
the difference.

But what do I feel? I wasn't sure of my
own feelings about my blindness. Or why
else would being called "handicapped"
bug me so?

Grandpa interrupted my thoughts. "Did
you hear about our new neighbors, the
Hollanders?"

"No, I haven't met them."

"You'll really take to the little
Hollander girl," he said. I heard him
unscrew the cap of his thermos.

"Why is that?"

Grandpa took a long drink and then
continued. "Because she's handicapped
like you. Well, not exactly like you.
Jennifer is her name, and she's in a
wheelchair. In fact—" he paused and
apparently looked up the street. "Yep,
she's sitting on her porch right now."

My face suddenly felt flushed, and I wondered if my cheeks were red. Why did I feel so funny? I should be excited about a new kid on Canwood Street.

I gathered my bag and started walking quickly. "Gotta go, Grandpa . . . I can't be late for school. Bye!"

"Why don't you say hi to Jennifer? I'm sure she'll see you walking by. Her house is the one before Mrs. Gardner's." Grandpa started his rake scratching on the lawn.

A new girl. In a wheelchair. She was . . . *handicapped*. Was she like one of those kids on a telethon? Was she retarded?

When I had walked up nearly half the block, I realized that I must be passing our new neighbor's house. I clenched my duffel bag and kept my head down. Even though I felt certain the new girl could see me from her front porch, I walked on by. When my radar picked up Mrs. Gardner's rosebush, I knew I was out of range. I felt guilty that I hadn't said hello.

All day at school I felt miserable. It didn't help that weirdo Alan was up to his usual antics. During lunchtime, while I was sitting with Judy, he passed behind me and said, "You don't want to sit there . . . not next to the handicapped girl." I couldn't eat any more of my sandwich.

Back in class, I couldn't get Alan and his remark off my mind. *The nerve of him,* I kept thinking. But then it dawned on me. . . .

The problem wasn't Alan. It wasn't even Grandpa Dudley. *You dummy. How could you be so blind?*

All the way home, I kept thinking about Matt and Chris, my mom and dad. Even Scrappy. They accepted me as I was. But did I? *I* knew who *really* had the problem.

I counted my steps to Mrs. Gardner's rosebushes. When my radar told me the bush was next to me, I reached out. Being careful of thorns, I ran my hand over the bush until I found a big bloom. It smelled so sweet. Hoping that Mrs. Gardner wouldn't mind, I snapped the stem. I held the rose tightly and continued on.

When my steps told me I was directly in front of our new neighbor's house, I gathered my courage. "Hello, is anyone home?" I called over the fence.

I heard a girl's voice from the direction of the porch. "Hi, I'm Jennifer. What's your name?"

I breathed a sigh of relief. "Aimee," I said. At that instant I heard Scrappy running up the sidewalk toward me. He bounded up and began whining and licking my arm. "And this is my dog, Scrappy."

"It's nice to meet you. I wish I had a dog."

Suddenly I remembered the rose. "May I give you something?" I asked as I opened the front gate. Slowly I made my way up the unfamiliar walk.

"The steps are right in front of you," Jennifer said. For some reason, it didn't bother me that someone like her— someone who was handicapped—was offering me some help.

I reached for the railing and carefully climbed all four of the front steps. "How did you know I couldn't see?"

"I have other friends who are blind," Jennifer said with a smile in her voice. "I've been in and out of hospitals a lot. I'm in a wheelchair."

I could tell that I was really going to like her.

"I've got red hair and blue eyes," Jennifer went on. "My wheelchair is blue, too."

It was nice of her to offer so much information. Again, I didn't seem to mind that she wanted to help.

"Oh, I almost forgot. This is for you." I held out the rose. She took the stem and I heard her sniff.

"Thank you," she said softly. After a pause she continued. "I saw you go by this morning. I'm glad you decided to stop. Sometimes it's, well—it's lonely."

"You mean being the new kid on the block?" I offered.

"Sometimes it's just lonely being . . . being handicapped. You must know what I mean?"

I knew exactly what she meant. For the first time, I thought I might have found someone who could understand exactly how I felt.

I nodded my head. "Yes, I know what you mean about being handicapped. I guess we've got a lot in common."

Handicapped. I had used the word to describe not only Jennifer, but myself. And I actually told someone in a wheelchair that I had things in common with her!

"I've got to go or my mom will wonder where I am. See you later," I said. Scrappy and I made our way back to the front walk.

"Bye," Jennifer called. "Thanks for the rose. And thanks for stopping."

"See you later." I waved good-bye.

I tousled Scrappy's hair and briskly walked toward home. The oak trees smelled wet and sweet. The roses were fragrant. The sky, I imagined, must be blue. I waved hello to Grandpa Dudley. Yes, Canwood Street was a wonderful place to live. I thought that everything was perfect before—Mrs. Gardner's roses, Mr. Espey's tomatoes, the oak trees, our friends. But now it was even more special. After all, not every street has two special, handicapped kids like Jennifer and me.

A VOICE FOR JAMIE

A church camp. How did *I* ever end up on a bus going to church camp? It would have been neater to go to a deaf camp with friends I could understand . . . friends who use sign language. But that's what I get for hanging around Kristen. She has a way of making me do things I think are icky.

And as we bounced along in an old church bus, the whole idea of spending a week with a bunch of her hearing girl friends at camp was bo-or-ring. I thought hearing girls were stuck up. They always think they're so much better, just because they can hear.

Oh, I guess I'd better introduce myself. My name is Jamie. I have a mop of brown curly hair, I like to read Laura Ingalls Wilder books, I love M & Ms, and I'm deaf. My friend Kristen, who could pass for my twin (except she likes Snickers bars), is deaf, too. We got to know each other at school. That's where Kristen cornered me and asked me to come to this church camp.

Anyway, Kristen and I are friends, maybe even best friends. We can both read lips, although I wish I were as good at lipreading as Kristen. And we're both super at sign language. At school we have races to see who can finger spell through the alphabet the fastest! The only thing I *don't* like about Kristen is, well . . . she's always talking about God. And she's always nice—even to hearing girls.

"Hey, Jamie." Kristen turned to me and spoke in sign language. *"You're going to love camp. And you'll really love Camille, our sign language interpreter. She's an awesome counselor. She even*

uses slang in her sign language . . . not like our English teachers at school!''

Suddenly we realized that someone was standing next to our seat. I looked up into the face of a girl with freckles and a French braid. She had been sitting across the aisle, watching Kristen and me sign to one another. Nervously, she shoved a message scrawled in pencil into Kristen's hands.

Can you guys teach me some signs?

''Sure, we'll teach you some signs,'' Kristen spoke up. The girl with freckles seemed surprised that Kristen could speak. ''And yes, we can read your lips . . . if you don't talk too fast or hide your mouth.'' Boy, Kristen sure has more guts than I do. I'm always afraid to use my voice, since I can't hear myself speak. And lots of times when I've tried to speak, I've gotten laughed at. I must sound funny.

"Wow, neat! What are you going to teach me?" the freckled girl asked, excitedly biting her nails. Actually, I didn't catch the first part of her sentence—I couldn't see her lips through her fingers. She had already flunked Kristen's first lesson! What an airhead.

Kristen, smiling and outgoing as ever, showed the girl how to finger spell her name. I watched Kristen's fingers slowly spell out M-A-R-C-I-E. Marcie was Freckle Face's name.

Marcie seemed thrilled with her new talent. She turned to the rest of her hearing friends at the front of the bus and proudly finger spelled.

Big deal, so she can finger spell her name, I thought. *Now Marcie will think she knows everything.*

She whipped back around and blurted another question. "Why do you two wear hearing aids if you can't hear me speak?"

What is this, deaf awareness week? I casually smoothed my hair over my ears. I thought I had done a good job of hiding my hearing aids when I combed my hair.

Kristen answered Marcie as if she had given this information a hundred times before. "Hearing aids," she said with a smile, "help us know when something's making a lot of noise . . . like this bus."

Or like you, Marcie, I thought.

Marcie half-stared at Kristen, letting the answer sink in. But she wasn't done. "What's it like being deaf?" she piped up. I glanced at her friends. They were flipping through comic books, but I could tell they were straining to hear.

Out of nowhere, I snapped, "WELL, WHAT'S IT LIKE BEING HEARING?"

Marcie took a step back as her friends shrank in their seats. "Wh-what was that?" Marcie asked, as if she didn't catch my words.

Oh, rats! *She didn't understand me.* I can't believe I even let sound come out of my mouth! Like I said, I hardly talk at all, especially around hearing girls. I probably sounded like a real nerd.

Kristen jumped in with a smile and an answer. "Marcie, you probably can't explain what it's like to hear . . . and we can't explain what it's like *not* to hear." Marcie and her friends seemed to relax a little.

Kristen, in her cheery way, kept talking. "Even though we can't hear, we enjoy lots of the same things you do. We can watch TV—"

Marcie flopped in her seat, leaned on her elbow, and said, "Wait a minute. If you can't hear, how can you enjoy, like,

'The Cosby Show'?'' We had to strain to read Marcie's lips because the bus was bouncing so much.

"Easy. Jamie and I have a decoder—a little box on top of the TV that sort of translates words into writing on the TV screen. Right, Jamie?" Kristen spoke and signed at the same time so I would be sure to understand. I just nodded, as if I could have cared less about TVs or decoders. It seemed to me that Marcie was being awfully nosy.

That didn't bother Kristen. With her same smile, she charged right ahead, "And we love to play charades and act out stories." Then Kristen got a bright idea. *"Hey, Jamie."* She turned to me and signed as she spoke. *"Do your impression of Bill Cosby dancing!"*

I shrugged my shoulders and gave her a dirty look, even though I didn't mean it. "Come on, Jamie," Kristen said out loud. "Please. Do that neat dance!"

Marcie jumped up. "Can you really dance like Bill Cosby? Let's see!" She was jabbering so fast I couldn't catch every word, but I got the idea.

"Yeah, Jamie, we love that crazy dance he does. Please!" Marcie's friends were kneeling on their seats, pleading.

Up until then, I had been pretty quiet around these dumb hearing girls. Here was my chance to show them I was as good as they were—if not better. Anyway, I *did* enjoy acting and imitating others. My deaf friends say I'm really good at impressions. I looked around, took a deep breath, and rose to my feet.

I don't know where I got the nerve, but I began my routine—twisting and jerking like Bill Cosby right there in the aisle of the bus. When I whirled around, I saw Marcie's friends sliding off their seats, laughing hysterically. I knew it! They weren't laughing with me. They were laughing *at* me! I threw myself back into my seat.

The bus jostled down the road as the laughter settled. Marcie still looked as though she was about to burst with questions. Finally she spoke up again.

"Kristen, are you ever sorry you can't hear?"

That time I caught every word on Marcie's lips. I quickly focused on Kristen. This was one answer I wanted to hear!

Kristen squinted, thinking, and then spoke. "Sometimes it's hard being deaf . . . but I'm not really . . . sorry. Besides, I feel closer to God." There was a long pause. I looked around at the girls in the bus and could tell that it was quiet.

The bus rounded a corner and turned onto a dirt road which bordered the edge of a woods. As we crested the hill we could see the camp, complete with bunk-houses, a meeting hall, a dining room, and a corral. Our bus pulled into a gravel parking lot and jerked to a stop. Before the driver could stand up and shout instructions, kids were climbing over each other to grab their sleeping bags, pillows, and jackets. Kristen and I reached for our things under the seat and piled out.

Immediately I saw a short, pretty blonde girl wave at Kristen. I figured she must be Camille, our interpreter. Hmmm. I wondered if she was as good at signing as Kristen claimed.

"Hi, Kristen," Camille signed and gave her a big hug. *"This must be your friend Jamie from school. Hi, Jamie!"* she signed at me.

"Yeah, hi," I sloppily signed back.

"Isn't it terrific being at camp?" Her fingers flew.

"We'll see," I signed, and then added, *"You can talk, you know. I can read lips. Not as well as Kristen does, but I'll manage."*

"Great! That's good to know!" Camille spoke up while signing at the same time. "Okay, girls, keep close to me so you can read my lips. I've got to organize this bunch of monkeys."

She laughed, looking at the rest of the kids who were slapping name tags on each other and passing around registration forms and pencils.

74

"Girls! Girls!" Camille yelled. "We have cabin assignments here!" In a few minutes Camille had the entire bus divided into neat groups. "And Marcie, you, Tracie, and Kelly are with Kristen and Jamie in my cabin. Got it?"

"Neat-o!" Marcie jumped up and down, clapping. "We're with you two," she shouted at Kristen and me.

Hearing kids . . . just who I wanted to room with.

I stuffed my sleeping bag under my arm and followed Kristen to our cabin. I was nearly pushed through the door by Tracie and Kelly, who raced to claim the best bunks. Tracie scrambled for one by the window. Kelly claimed the top bunk in the corner. Marcie quickly sat down on the bed nearest the bathroom. I tossed my sleeping bag on the bunk that was left. I could tell this was going to be a rowdy cabin.

I pulled some jeans and sweat shirts out of my duffel bag and folded them in one of the dresser drawers. Kristen was talking in sign language with Camille, their fingers flying a mile a minute. Why was Kristen always so disgustingly happy? And how could she trust Camille so much—someone who could *hear?*

As Camille helped the others unpack, I cornered Kristen. I didn't want anybody to eavesdrop, so I spoke only in sign language.

"Something's been bothering me ever since the bus ride."

Kristen seemed surprised. *"What's the matter?"*

"What's the big deal about God? You're deaf, Kristen. You're supposed to be mad at Him." I glanced over my shoulder to make sure Camille was nowhere in sight.

"I don't know how to explain it, Jamie," Kristen answered. *"You're deaf, too. You know what it's like. . . . It's quieter. So much other stuff is blocked out—my little brother's whining . . . people complaining . . . even my parents arguing. So I can 'hear' God better."*

76

She pointed to her ears. *"Do you know what I mean?"*

I looked at my friend sadly. No, I didn't know what she meant.

"Let's go check out the camp on our way to dinner," Camille announced while signing to Kristen and me.

The girls kicked their suitcases under the bunks, grabbed their sweat shirts, and bolted out the door.

I knotted my sweat shirt sleeves around my waist and followed. We headed for the swimming pool and stuck our toes in the water. From there we took a path to the stables and fed carrots to the horses. We passed by the meeting hall and pressed our noses against the windows to get a good look. Once again, Marcie was babbling off a lot of questions.

"What a motor mouth that girl is," I signed to Kristen as we stood directly in front of Marcie. Miss Freckle Face could have no idea what I was saying about her in our secret language.

Kristen quickly grabbed my fingers

with one hand and signed to me with the other. *"Hey . . . let's not gossip. Marcie's really trying."*

I felt a little ashamed. I knew it was wrong to say nasty things in sign language in front of somebody.

From the meeting hall, we headed toward the dining room. Our group played follow-the-leader—a dumb game Kristen obviously enjoyed playing with her hearing friends. I tagged behind.

The dining room was a big log cabin with elk horns and deer heads hung on the walls. Kids were everywhere. I stuck close to Kristen.

During dinner, Marcie had more questions. "Are my lips easy to read, Kristen?"

"Well, let's see . . ." Kristen examined Marcie's lips. "Yeah, your upper lip isn't too short . . . and you don't mumble. I'd say you're easy to lip read."

Except when your mouth is full of spaghetti, I thought as I watched her

78

chew. I wasn't kidding.

Everybody was chewing, so I just kept to myself. Although Camille often put down her knife and fork to sign, she got distracted with Tracie and Kelly, who were throwing peas at each other. The only one I felt comfortable with was Kristen.

That night we were in the bathroom getting ready for bed. Kristen and I were about to brush our teeth when I noticed Tracie and Kelly looking at us. In fact, Tracie started to say something to Kristen and me and then halfway through her sentence, she put her hand over her mouth. She didn't *want* us to read her lips! I quickly looked the other way and started squeezing toothpaste on my brush.

Just then Kelly started mouthing something else at us, but we had no idea what she was saying—her mouth was stuffed full of toothpaste. They were doing it just to be mean.

"Cut it out, you guys!" Marcie angrily punched Tracie on the shoulder. She turned to Kelly and threatened, "I'm going to tell Camille on you!"

I kept brushing my teeth, pretending nothing had happened. But inside I was fighting back tears. Then I shot a look at Kristen, and I couldn't believe my eyes.

Kristen was laughing. She was laughing at Tracie and Kelly. Then she started flinging toothpaste at them! That gave Tracie and Kelly more giggles. Kristen signed at them, *"You two have toothpaste for brains!"* Of course, they had no idea what she was saying. The two of them stood there looking confused and a little angry.

Kristen shook her finger at them and then spoke up, "I just wanted to give you an idea of how it feels to be left out. Teasing can hurt." But she smiled as she spoke.

I was amazed. Kristen had handled the whole thing like a pro.

Camille entered the bathroom. "Okay, what's going on, you guys?"

"Oh, nothing. Just a little fun,"

Kristen answered. Tracie and Kelly had sheepish looks on their faces.

"Okay, then. Let's get it together for cabin time," Camille said, clapping. She turned to me, and I tried to hide my hurt feelings. *"Anything wrong?"* she signed, putting her arm around me and giving me a squeeze. I shook my head no.

During cabin time, some of the girls sat on the edge of their bunks, while others sat cross-legged on the floor. I lay on my side in bed, my eyes mostly on Camille. She joked with everyone, even Kristen and me. We played games, and she asked a lot of questions like what was going on at school, who had the worst little brother, and what happened last week on Saturday morning cartoons. I could see why Kristen loved Camille, and why she trusted her. And she was right—Camille definitely didn't sign like our English teachers at school!

Marcie showed how she could finger spell not only her name, but everybody's name in the whole cabin. I thought back on the bathroom scene. It struck me that at least Marcie was making an effort. And I realized something else—I had made no effort at all.

Cabin time began to quiet down. Camille, sitting cross-legged on her bed, opened her Bible. I settled in for something superboring.

"Prayer is so neat," Camille signed and spoke. "It's our way of talking to God. And isn't it great that He actually listens? And that He understands sign language, too?" She winked at Kristen and me.

Hmm, I never thought of that before.

"But conversation is two-way. We have to hear Him, too. How do we do that?" Camille asked.

Marcie raised her hand. "By reading the Bible."

"That's right. But more than just reading, we have to really *listen*. That's the only way to have good communication. Look here." Camille pointed to the Bible on her lap. " 'I am the Good Shepherd. I know My sheep and My sheep know Me. . . . They will *listen* to My voice.' "

Marcie was scratching her head, thinking. Kelly was staring at the ceiling. Tracie was examining her toes. Kristen had a faraway look on her face, as though she understood exactly what Camille was reading.

Do they hear His voice? What does it sound like? I strained to hear what Kristen seemed to hear. Then I rolled over on my bunk and sighed. *There's no voice talking to me.*

A couple days later Camille took us on a nature walk. I couldn't stop thinking about hearing God's voice. We passed by a grove of pines. The wind was moving the branches, but I couldn't hear the pines whispering as I had read they did in one of Laura Ingalls Wilder's books. We spied a woodpecker attacking an oak tree. I saw his beak drilling like a jackhammer, but I could only imagine the sound. Camille led us beside a big waterfall and covered her ears as though the water was making a loud roar. But I wasn't certain what "roar" meant, either. After all, lions roar. Does a waterfall sound like a lion?

Later on we put on our swimsuits and headed for the pool. The hearing girls played Marco Polo, but I sat on a lounge chair and watched. I couldn't hear anyone shout "Marco!", so how could I play?

Kristen came and sat next to me. *"It's hard not being able to play, isn't it?"* she signed.

I leaned on my wrists and nodded. A long stretch of silence hung between us.

Kristen suddenly sat up. *"Jamie, I forgot to tell you. Tonight is team competition night, and I heard we're going to play charades. Let's you and I surprise everybody!"*

Charades! I didn't want to admit it, but instantly I was on pins and needles. Kristen was right—we would wow 'em!

After supper the log and timber meeting hall was jam-packed with groups from every cabin. Teams were competing in every corner of the room. I couldn't hear what was going on, but it seemed like there was a lot of noise in the hall. Our corner was ready to go.

We knelt in a huddle across from the opposing team. Everybody was scribbling ideas on paper, poking one another and whispering. I could tell that the other cabins must be coming up with some good ideas for charades. Several times the girls rolled over, giggling and clapping.

Camille stood between our two teams and blew a whistle. First up was Marcie. She walked over to the other group to take her slip of paper. She unfolded it, read the message, and stuffed the paper in her pocket, rolling her eyes.

"Come on, Marcie," Tracie called. Kristen and I grinned at each other. We were ready to guess.

Camille clicked her stopwatch, and Marcie nervously began to act out her charade. She stretched and swayed, her arms floating like . . . *branches of a tree*

. . . a . . . willow tree! Just to make
certain, I quickly signed to Kristen what I
thought was the answer. Her face lit up
and she nodded quickly.

I jumped to my feet and whipped out
the answer in sign language. *"Wind in the
Willows!"*

"Jamie's answer is *The Wind in the
Willows!"* Camille shouted the
interpretation.

Marcie jumped up and down like a
kangaroo. I was right! Everybody on my

team patted my shoulders. Camille announced our time—twenty seconds.

A girl with curly black hair rose from the opposing team, walked over to us, and took a slip of paper. She studied her message as she went back to her team. When the whistle blew and the stopwatch started, she began playacting her charade. Twenty . . . thirty . . . almost sixty seconds passed before her team finally guessed correctly—*Charlie and the Chocolate Factory.*

Once again, our team was on. It was Kelly's turn. She skipped in a circle and whistled, leaning over and patting us all on our heads. *She looks like . . . "Snow White and the Seven Dwarfs."* Again I was quick to my feet. "'Snow White and the Seven Dwarfs,'" I spoke out loud before my hands even started to sign. *Good grief, I spoke out loud!*

Several girls on the other team collapsed against each other, whining and moaning.

"Hurray for Jamie!" Marcie, Kristen,

Kelly, and Tracie danced around me.

"Boy, Jamie, you are absolutely amazing!" Kelly said, as she shook my shoulders. Kristen had to interpret that sentence for me—Kelly was shaking me so hard, her lips looked like jiggling Jell-O!

Our teams went back and forth, acting out the charades and guessing as quickly as we could. After the third round, it was my turn. I unfolded my slip of paper and read my charade. I knew exactly how it should be acted out.

I walked up to my team, took a deep breath, and waited for Camille to give the signal. Then I acted as though I were primping in front of a mirror, putting on lipstick and admiring myself like Miss America. The next minute I was hunched and snarling, acting like a werewolf.

" 'Beauty and the Beast'!" Kristen jumped up and shouted. Hurray! I knew Kristen would do it. If anybody could understand my body language, it was definitely my deaf friend!

An hour passed quickly. It was no contest—our cabin won the entire team competition night! We grabbed each other and bounced up and down, dancing in a circle. I couldn't hear the applause, but I could feel it. I saw everyone's mouth moving, and I knew they were shouting and laughing.

I also knew they weren't laughing at me.

The girls began stomping and chanting, "We're number one. We're number one!" I felt the vibrations all through me, and I stomped right in time with them. "We're number one!" Kristen was yelling. I found myself shouting, too, "We're number one!" I couldn't believe I was having so much fun using my voice! I wasn't embarrassed. I didn't care what I sounded like. For the first time since I got off the camp bus, I was glad that Kristen had talked me into coming.

I looked up and noticed Camille. Our eyes met for a moment, and I thought I saw tears in her eyes. For a split second, it didn't matter that I couldn't hear and others could.

After the winners were announced and refreshments were served, all the kids left the meeting hall and walked over to the campfire. Kristen and I strolled together. Suddenly, Marcie came from behind and flung her arms around each of us. We found an empty log and sat, huddling together with the rest of the girls from our cabin.

The kids quieted down, the camp speaker stood up, and Camille positioned herself to interpret the message. Kristen pulled her flashlight out of her jacket and focused it on Camille. Neither of us wanted to miss a single word. For the first time I actually wanted to hear what someone had to say about the Bible. I glanced around the campfire. Everybody else seemed warm and happy to be there, too.

Camille's hands moved like a windmill as she signed the speaker's words. " *What do you think? If a man has a hundred sheep and one wanders away from the rest, won't he leave the ninety-nine on the hillside and set out to look for the one who has wandered away? Yes, and if he should chance to find it, I assure you he is more delighted over that one than he is over the ninety-nine who never wandered away.' "*

I looked over at Kristen, who smiled at me.

" 'You can understand, then, that it is never the will of your Father in heaven that a single one of these little ones should be lost.' " The speaker paused and closed her Bible. Camille rested her hands, waiting for her to continue. *"Have you ever felt lost before? Well, if you have, listen for God's voice. He not only cares about the whole flock, but He cares for you."*

I felt even warmer inside, and I knew it wasn't because of the fire. The speaker began to pray. The kids around us bowed their heads and closed their eyes. Kristen and I fixed our eyes on Camille's hands to hear what the speaker was praying.

After the fire died down into glowing embers, we all stretched, yawned, and began to wander back to our cabins. I watched Kristen massage Camille's arm muscles. Our poor interpreter was zonked from so much signing.

Camille smiled at me, and the truth hit—even though there were far many more hearing kids at camp, Camille cared for *me*. Just as if I were that single lost sheep.

Tracie and Kelly were walking ahead of me. One of them jabbed the other in the ribs, whispered, and then stopped to turn around.

''We're, uh . . . . sorry about what happened in the bathroom, Jamie.'' Tracie exaggerated her words too much.

I shrugged my shoulders and nodded. Before, I would have gloated over such an apology. Now I realized it was no big deal. The toothpaste incident seemed like ages ago. Like Kristen, I was beginning to feel . . . quieter inside. More peaceful.

I stopped along the dirt path and listened to the quiet. The trees moved, and the wind touched my face. I stopped imagining what whispering pines must sound like. Instead, I began to enjoy the quiet. Not just around me, but *inside* of me. Perhaps, after all, God's voice was talking to me, too.

Back at the cabin, most of the girls were already in their bunks. It was dark, so I couldn't tell if anyone was talking, but it didn't matter. I had a lot to think about. Camille hugged me and Kristen, and we crawled into our bunks.

After lights out, when I was sure that almost everyone was asleep, I shined my flashlight on the ceiling, a signal to Kristen that I wanted to tell her something. When I saw her flashlight twinkle back, I stuffed mine between my knees and moved my hands in the beam of light.

"For the first time, I can hear God."

Wasn't it fun getting to know my friends? Were you surprised (and maybe a little embarrassed) when Josh fell out of his wheelchair? How do you think Jamie felt when the girls at camp made fun of her? And wasn't it neat that Aimee could tell which socks she had on by feeling them? (Try standing in front of your closet, closing your eyes, and touching the sleeves and collars of your shirts. Can you guess which ones are which?)

I learned that Kristen, Josh, and the rest were just everyday sorts of people, very much like you. They have the same fearful feelings, the same sense of right and wrong, the same love for games and surprises, and the very same ability to reach out to God and others.

Do you remember the apostle Paul in the Bible? He had a disability, although we don't know what it was. And guess what he said? ''I can do all things through Christ who gives me strength'' (Philippians 4:13). It doesn't matter whether we're in a wheelchair or can do the best cartwheel in school—we all have times when we feel afraid, have doubts, or do something stupid. But like the kids in these stories, I know you, too, can do many more things than you ever dreamed possible.

Wouldn't you like to be friends with someone like Josh or Aimee? You can! You may know someone in your own neighborhood—someone who is disabled—who would like to be your friend. I just know you won't be as shy about meeting that person, now that you've met my friends in this book.

Try it—give someone your smile and warm hello. If you're afraid, just ask God to help you. It may be the start of an exciting new adventure!

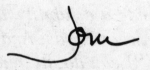